4.

To the Rivins

Drew Baurgalupa

Journal of an Itinerant Artist

Journal of an Itinerant Artist

DREW BACIGALUPA

Much of the material in this book first appeared in Viva, the Sunday magazine supplement of the Santa Fe New Mexican.

Cover and title page designed by James E. McIlrath.

ISBN: 0-87973-887-1
Library of Congress Catalog Card Number: 77-78739

Published, printed, and bound in the U.S.A. by
Our Sunday Visitor, Inc., Noll Plaza, Huntington, Indiana 46750

887

For Ellen,
and for our children—
Gian Andrea, Pier Francesca,
Ruan Saire, Chiara Domenica,
and Daria Concessa

PREFACE

IN THE THIRD DECADE of the twentieth century, long before television in the home, and during a Depression that precluded costly entertainments, I often sat at the feet of elders and listened to their tales. Grandparents, parents, uncles and aunts, other relatives, and friends —in telling me about themselves and about loved ones, they began my own lengthy quest for identity.

But this tradition today has faltered, or is practiced (almost exclusively) on professional analytic couches. Our frenetic pace permits little time for the telling of tales or family histories. Our children are ignorant of who and what their parents are. Perhaps it was mainly for that reason that I began writing these essays. They first appeared in a local Sunday newspaper, and the many requests I have received for a collection of them suggest that this book is justified.

"There Is a Season for All Things." Believing that, I have placed the tales within the format of the liturgical calendar. But I have made no attempt to be chronological or sequential.

Drew Bacigalupa
Santa Fe

DECEMBER

But now, as I hold Clare's card,
its bright design prompts me
to utter the word aloud—
Magi.

WE ACQUIRED the puppy on the first day of Advent. She is five weeks old and, missing the warmth of her mother, cries through the initial night under our roof. But from the moment we met her, she chose us rather than our having chosen her, toddling away from the gamboling litter to snuggle against the feet of my wife, then going in turn to each of our children. She has entered our hearts; we have a dog.

"You should call her Maranatha," a friend facetiously suggests, "in commemoration of the day you got her." It is an Aramaic-Greek word heralding Christmas, repeated in liturgies at this time of year. The family considers quite a few names for nearly a week, but in the end the dog is "Mara." We feel comfortable with the abbreviation, content that we have not abused a word usually reserved for use in sacred contexts, while acknowledging that this creature came to us in the awesome season of preparation, expectancy, and hope.

Christmas seems a remote abstraction at the desert resort motel where I am lodged for an early December conference. The banquet halls at evening feature elegantly jeweled and baubled trees. Tanned, glittering socialites sing drunken parodies of traditional carols during the wee small hours before dawn. Nothing more. The resort is a planet unto itself, insulated against everything but luxury and indulgence.

Two enormous pools flanked by towering palms are its heart; in and around them, the rich sun themselves, eat and drink, close business deals, and begin or conclude erotic adventures. I stare at obese trade tycoons floating in steaming thermal baths, bikinied mistresses in attendance with the best of booze and heavy trays of gourmet snacks.

Once the sun is down, the palms are spotlighted, fountains splash in neon splendor, and dozens of flaming torches illuminate the gargantuan Cecil B. De Mille setting. Is it the American Dream come true, this posh Hollywood in the desert, this privileged soundstage designed for hedonistic pleasure? Is it Eden, the garden of Allah, a glimpse of Paradise? Or only vulgar and—in these days of "energy crisis" and a groping toward austerity—criminal? I leave my bed one late hour and walk around a deserted poolside, the lights and fountains and torches all mine, burning away exclusively for me, a pharaoh shielded against all meanness beyond these perimeters. I utter aloud "Obscenity" and look to the heavens for cleansing. But the orange lights on the great royal palms blot out the sky beyond; I cannot see the full moon, nor, certainly, an Eastern Star to guide me.

Work sessions of the conference are held at a nearby religious community, a refreshingly modest complex of buildings at the foot of scorched mountains. Among the first words of greeting I hear are "Maranatha, the Lord Cometh," from delegates assembled to question and to work hopefully toward resolving problems of liturgical renewal. They are the foremost authorities on liturgy from across the country, men and women of various Christian denominations, ministers and priests and laity, each a recognized expert in a particular field.

The atmosphere is highly charged, strong personalities jockeying for position, famous scholars competing for precious, rationed minutes of erudition. There are moments when I'm convinced the conference has floundered on a reef of non-productive, ceaseless talk, is hopelessly mired in a paralytic sea of rhetoric, theory, and academia. But I prefer it to the nearby oasis with my opulent room.

And at the closing liturgy, I hear participants express aloud in petitions of prayer their own anxieties over scholarship: "Spare us the stigma of intellectual imperialists," "Help us translate words into action among the people and for their good." On this last day they are less proud, less impatient, more reflective. The sense of waiting—Advent—is among them. I overhear a whispered comment that perhaps this conference was not in vain.

At home, the children greet me with lengthy reports on Mara. She has stopped whimpering in the night, is eating heartily, has grown, and is more mischievous. They lavish love and play on the puppy, plan training and discipline for her, anticipate her behavior among the paraphernalia and trappings of tree and gifts. They discuss her name with their mother and me; and over dinner, by the light of candles gracing an Advent wreath, we speak of the Aramaic-Greek phrase, its seasonal use, its implicit meaning of waiting and expectancy of deferred joy. Our four-year-old has problems with the conversation and suddenly blurts out, "I can't wait! Mara's a Christmas present, and I want all of Christmas now!" Her older sister, touching the puppy's head, argues eloquently. "She's not a Christmas present but an Advent present. And she's got to wait—with us—for Christmas morning."

OUR MAIL is always heavy; but in the few weeks before Christmas, it is staggering. Season's greetings come in by the dozens, from all over the world, many from old friends we haven't seen in a quarter century. Cards arrive from mail-order clients we've never met, or tourists who were in our gallery only once; from people we've known briefly at national workshops and conventions, or met on vacations. Forgetful of names, I must ask my wife: Who is this, when was that, do we know him?

The cards are corralled in a huge wooden bowl, and each day they pile higher, eventually spilling over. Some of the signatures on them remain faceless to me, but names have become familiar through yearly repetition. A few are from my army buddies and wartime friends, their names on cards surrounded by those of total strangers—wives and children and even grandchildren.

I sometimes think the enormous trough of cards is like a disorganized notebook for an epic Tolstoian novel. Many of the greetings include lengthy notes and long newsletters advising us of births and deaths, marriages and divorces, professional advances or setbacks, relocations and travel. Children we've never met have grown up on those scribbled pages.

We are always too busy before Christmas to peruse the cards at leisure. But in those rare still and quiet moments, perhaps early morning while the rest of the family sleeps, one of us will pause before that towering mound and turn over the cards until one demands attention.

Here is Clare's, as brief and taciturn as ever. I'm aware of the discipline and effort required of him to write anything. So much easier to neglect correspondence and hope our paths will cross again—against the bar at O'Hare probably, between planes in Chicago.

We spent a memorable pre-Christmas week together in '44 at Southampton, though neither of us can lay claim to having seen that great port. We arrived on troop trucks in dark and fog and were herded inside a public park that had been converted into a fenced, guarded, tented debarkation area for France. Blackout and persistent fog prevented us from seeing anything beyond a few yards. We could hear trams and, somewhere outside the perimeters of the park, shoppers, bells, broadcasts of Christmas music. Even daylight hours, locked in fog, gave us no glimpse of anything beyond our tents.

Quatermaster stores were low, we were told, cigarettes and liquor unavailable. A rumor persisted that that was not the case, that supplies were being channeled to the black market. I remember Clare, a chain-smoker, searching in the rutted, frozen mud for discarded butts. There was mutinous talk among the men of going over the fence, raiding officers' quarters—anything to get tobacco and a drop of Christmas cheer.

One night we passed the chaplain's tent and heard soldiers inside caroling. The sound was unreal, a sweet sanity no longer relevant to anything we knew. Clare and I walked on. And when, inevitably, the air-raid sirens wailed, we felt a sense of propriety at this return to normalcy. Carols, sentiment, brotherly love—these seemed blasphemous at that time, in that place.

Yet, something more than privation of cigarettes and drink tore at Clare's insides. The dreariness of the camp, the men's surliness, and the sounds of Southampton out beyond the fog kept his nerves raw and his face hard. We silently stomped the ruts together, fighting cold, fighting thoughts of the season. I observed him ministering roughly, with a harsh and angry tenderness, to young green recruits at the breaking point.

Late Christmas Eve, while men huddled morosely about tent stoves, I became aware that Clare had been missing since dusk. And I guessed where. He eventually appeared in the canvas doorway, broad-grinned, his arms piled high with gifts—cartons of cigarettes, boxes of chocolates, and bottles of brandy. The black-market rumors had proved true —and the storehouse vulnerable.

If we thought it then, as merriment spread throughout the camp, we failed to say so. But now, as I hold Clare's card, its bright design prompts me to utter the word aloud—Magi.

I SIT with a group of friends for whom the approach of Christmas poses a threat. One of them fears holiday drunkenness and the seasonal

binge of her husband. Another speaks of his children's annual disappointment in their gifts, which can't possibly measure up to the glam-
orous commercial come-ons. An elderly woman, who lives alone, says
it is an especially vicious time of year for those without family or
friends. Someone suggests that the holidays are always a time of catharsis, when our anxieties are released in spasms of undisciplined behavior. Suicide statistics soar. A religious man feels that without reli-
gion, without faith, Christmas never meets our Great Expectations.
We are bitter over the absence of liberating joy, which tradition and
culture have led us to expect.

From more than one circle of friends, I hear the groan of despair.
How, with Watergates, rampant crime, continuing international wars,
punishing economic inflation, an energy crisis, and—especially—the
collapse of moral and ethical codes, can anyone believe we behave as
Christians or that the word and the feast have any meaning at all to
modern man? Shouldn't we, finally, admit that some primordial need
forces us, like the savages and pagans before us, to acknowledge the
solstice with a Saturnalian bash; and stop kidding ourselves that the
holiday in late twentieth century means anything more?

An obstacle to my accepting this argument is the existence of the
two children born of our marriage during my middle years. No matter
what despairs I bring home from a battered and cynical adult world,
they greet them with shining eyes, innocence, naïveté, and the simple
belief that life is good and Christmas is coming. It is not merely the
magic spell of a fairy tale for them. The older child already knows the
secret of Santa Claus; knows too that the historical Christ entered a
world much less romantic than the tinseled greeting cards. That
doesn't seem to matter. The children know in their hearts, instinctively, that something profound—and good—happens to man at Christ-
mastime.

Don Lorenzo knew it, too. He was a child in no sense, long passed
beyond innocence and illusion, harsh as any man I've known. In his

late fifties when I knew him, father to a young friend of mine, he was a short, thickset man of many moods, who frequently brooded and occasionally erupted with fierce outbursts of temper. He had retired from city life and lived at the family's country farm, joined in the summer and over winter holidays by his wife and large clutch of noisy, brilliant, stimulating children.

At first intimidated by his roughness—his angers, profanities, and blasphemies—I grew close to him, in time, sharing his fondness for wine from his own vineyard, for taking long walks over the fields of Tuscany, and for conversation. At some point during each of my visits to the farm with his fun-loving son, Don Lorenzo and I would desert the elegant country parlor, where family and friends dazzled each other with wit, and tramp across the fields, his handsome, faithful setters always nearby. Don Lorenzo was not a reticent man, and I came to know him well.

He mistrusted practically everyone and everything. Governments were universally corrupt—to be despised at all times, and resisted whenever possible. Schools were disastrous, producing charming aristocratic intellectuals like his own sons and daughters or blundering civil servants from the middle class, but never educating anyone. The church was a confused bureaucracy managed by spoiled children lining their pockets while lecturing him on the wrong of natural, God-given appetites. People for the most part were no damned good, too sentimental or too brutal, too selfish or piously altruistic, too complaining or long-suffering. He *knew*—he was as bad as the rest, had violated every commandment, and wallowed in all the evils.

He had lost or been abandoned by everyone he'd ever loved. Those whom death hadn't claimed in disgusting disease or futile wars, society had stolen from him through existential philosophy and changing mores. His wife was alienated from him by an identity crisis and sexual confusion that neither of them understood; children were building lives, in the new way, divorced from parents; mistresses used him as pragmatically as he used them. Once, as we readied for a summer swim in a swollen river, he removed his clothing in a slow and precise ritual. And perhaps the wine spoke: "Life's like preparing to swim. It strips us of everything."

I remember much, and have forgotten much, that Don Lorenzo said. But this year, with the prophets of Humbug proclaiming Christmas a falsehood while my little girls glow with promise and hope, I remember a Midnight Eve and Don Lorenzo free of anguish, open and tolerant. I goaded him about the crack in his hide and mercilessly reminded him of the bitter remark on the river bank. "I should have qualified that," he said. "Life strips us of *nearly* everything. But Christ was born, and did live, and did die. No one can take that away from me."

JANUARY

But he gave me, I think, just a glimpse
into the tough and true nature of
sainthood.

THE LITTLE children have been very patient in withholding the Magi from their tabletop crèche all through the holidays. But now that Epiphany's here, they line up Balthazar, Gaspar, and Melchior, and express a renewed interest in the Nativity scene—of first priority through Christmas Eve, but a bit neglected once the bright packages appeared under the tree.

Our youngest child is curious about those strange-sounding gifts the kings bear. I try to explain the symbolism of their giving, but she is soon distracted. I watch her run after the puppy, who has appropriated her new toy; then I turn to an after-dinner brandy in my hand. I close my eyes, let the aroma permeate my senses, and, relaxing, allow buried images to surface.

We had no brandy snifter, but swilled the cognac from an upturned bottle. And there was precious little of it for three men. Clare and I had conned a young corporal into sharing the last of his gift from an officer, presented to him for performing some humiliating orderly duty. The corporal was soft and homesick, and the brutal holidays had pained him grievously. A sensitive and orthodox boy, he suffered more than most of us, missing the rituals he'd grown up with in rural Pennsylvania, terrified of the horrors on all sides, shocked as much by personal moral collapse as by the immorality of war itself. Even now, as he tried to speak of Epiphany while Clare and I argued the availability of more cognac, the corporal was staring from a chateau-tower window of our quarters, across snow-blanketed fields, at a tent in the distance. A long line of men, francs in hand, huddled forlornly on the ice, waiting their turns to enter that flimsy, pitiable structure. And inside, the timorous corporal had heard as well as we, was a fourteen-year-old girl from the nearby village.

Clare was holding out. He had some Calvados stashed away somewhere—he always had something—but this day, without denying a hidden reserve, he resolutely refused to produce it. The lines of his face were tauter than ever, his usual rough humor absent. When I continued to press him about the drink, he unleashed a fury of profanities, saying there were all kinds of untagged wounded, and he was one of them. The liquor was the only medication he could count on, 100-proof guarantee of escape when he needed it. Maybe even a passport to sanity. He was through sharing the booze or anything else with anyone. From this day forward, he would concentrate on survival of Number One. What he had, he'd keep.

I spent the afternoon working alone in Battalion Headquarters, our field cases and equipment set up haphazardly in the main salon of the once-elegant chateau. Obscene graffitti left behind by Germans who'd used the house before us glared down from paneled walls. Stacks of paperwork, much of it concerning personnel, needed my attention. The outfit had been together three years, and most of the names on reports before me were of men I'd known well at one time or another. It was impossible to lose their faces in the statistics of blundering accidents, illness, madness, and death. I was convinced that afternoon that the war would never end and that none of us would come out of it alive.

Clare had intercepted a mail-call and brought in a few letters. We stood before a roaring fire on the huge marble hearth and quietly read. Each letter I opened brought word of new deaths, deaths of childhood or school friends, neighbors, cousins, in the Pacific, in the Mediterranean, under the bombs of London or on these fields of France. And the last was worst of all—a sister's fiancé whom I held dear and had hoped to meet on furlough within a month, killed in a paratrooper training exercise when his glider disintegrated over Britain. This final, unacceptable blow must have blazoned across my face. For no words passed between us, but Clare stared at me with deep concern; he unhitched the canteen from his cartridge belt, removed its cap, and placed the flask in my hands. It was full to the brim with Calvados, his guarded reserve, his passport to sanity.

Later, when the canteen was emptied and I had wandered aimlessly, blindly, over the frozen fields surrounding the chateau, when I had collapsed in a deep drift and surrendered gratefully to oblivion, Clare moved in from the distance at which he had shadowed me. He lugged me back to quarters and silently sat watch by the fire while I slept.

"But what are frankincense and myrrh? And why did the kings bring those?" daughter Daria is asking. Staring into the golden liquid in the brandy glass, pondering the nature of gifts, I do not immediately answer. And then the child is gone again, off on a merry chase through other rooms of the house, and I hear her loud, clear laughter with brothers and sisters.

TWO LADIES, working wives and mothers at a table next to mine in the coffee shop, loudly argue the pros and cons of Women's Liberation. One of them thinks that careers outside the home are essential to personal fulfillment; the other is tired of balancing employment against domestic responsibilities, insists that the truly liberated woman is the one free to remain at home. I keep my eyes glued on a newspaper, hoping to betray no interest in their treacherous conversation. The last time I ventured into this topical no-man's land, one of my sisters reminded me that I'm not qualified to have opinions about subjugated women. "All you've known—all your life—are liberated women."

And (she might have added) the family had a tradition of independent females long before she and I arrived on the scene. We never knew our mother's mother except in photographs (she died before her children married), but grandmother Concetta was nevertheless a real and vital force in our lives. She was too strong to be obliterated by death; stories about her persist on two continents even today. I never felt cheated of her—her spirit always surfaced whenever friends and relatives who loved (or hated) her got together.

Concetta was notorious in turn-of-the-century Baltimore as a woman who didn't know her place. Poor though she was, she had the best-dressed kids on the block by diligently sewing the latest fashions from the finest cloth she could afford. Her frame home, modest but occasionally featured in the tabloids as another George-Washington-Slept-Here site, boasted tasteful furnishings and strict order. Highly competitive and striving to be best at everything, she drew envy from neighbor women less meticulous about running a home. But it was outside the house, in the streets where Concetta's boundless energy drove her, that she was censured by men and women alike.

They say she went on late errands of mercy, lantern in hand, in a place where and at a time when respectable women did not venture out alone. She nursed the sick and dying, relative, friend, or foe; she shocked fastidious friends by carrying charity, food and clothing, to the destitute and social outcasts; she spent countless nights away from husband and children, helping bring infants into the world or preparing the dead for the grave; she was a self-appointed, one-member vice squad, elbowing her way into brawling bars and smoke-filled backrooms to collar a man squandering his paycheck on drink and gambling; she shouldered many of those men shamefaced through the old port, back to their families.

It is sworn that once, seeing on the street a small girl clothed in a dress copied exactly from one of Concetta's original designs for her own daughter, my grandmother lifted the child off her feet, carried her to the nearest puddle, and dropped her in it. On another occasion, an unlucky dog-catcher, holding Concetta's pet terrier captive in his arms blocks away from her house, was accosted by her with broom in hand. One sharp rap across his head made the man release the dog, which went scampering home on command.

When I had soldiered a war and almost finished my formal education, I went for the first time to my grandmother's birthplace, Meta de Sorrento. No one there had forgotten her. An old priest, exclaiming *"Aime!"* and crossing himself at mention of her name, told me what a scandalous young woman she had been. In days when ladies did not raise their voices in public, Concetta strummed the mandolin and sang loud enough for all the peninsula to hear. Worse, she danced, when, God knows, only the men did the ritual dances. Even worse (*madonna santa!*), she swam in the sea while good women of the town avoided the beaches because rough fishermen worked or pleasured there. The aged cleric studied me carefully, seeking the genetic taint she surely must have bequeathed to her grandchildren.

I had gone to Sorrento to find Concetta's sister, Vincenza, who, everyone said, "should have been your grandmother." Vincenza was the one secretly wooed by my grandfather, and to whom he sent passage to come to America as his bride. But she could not endure leaving her family, nor face the prejudices and terrors heaped on immigrants from across the sea. Vincenza showed the letter and the boat ticket to her sister, Concetta. A bust photograph of the young man, who was not from Sorrento but outside town, "over the mountain," portrayed him as not only handsome but "looking intelligent and with honest eyes." Concetta picked up the boat ticket along with the stranger's photograph, and started packing.

I have always felt as close to her as if she actually lived during my lifetime, and taught me at her knee a thing or two about toughness and courage and being a rebel. Something the scandalized priest at Meta de Sorrento said causes me to think that she could make sense of Women's Liberation (or any other cause). Looking down at the sea where she flagrantly swam under the disapproving eyes of the entire town, he mumbled sadly, using the present tense almost as if he were back in those faraway days: "It'll be better when she's gone to America—a New World for a new kind of young woman. She disturbs us here too much. She tells me in my own church—and anyone else who'll listen—that she's got to be herself, she can't conform. Even so, I'm going to miss her. And always wonder about her special gifts, and why we here are too timid to accept them."

TOURISTS in our gallery are often astonished to discover that the man next to them in walking shorts and sandals, hippie-bearded and mouthing slang, is a priest. Or that the miniskirted gal, as revealed by her conversation, is a nun who has kicked the habit. Because we specialize in liturgical arts, the gallery attracts many religious of all denominations. Those who do not look, act, or speak in the stereotyped manner that many of us in this country still believe is appropriate, cause minor scandal. A schoolteacher from Kansas, having listened to a minister utter a mild oath of praise over a religious painting, clucks disapprovingly at his departing back.

It must be the Puritan ethic of America that sustains such an unrealistic attitude. Certainly in Europe, especially in Mediterranean countries, clergymen are not expected to be plaster saints. In fact, their peccadillos are often cherished as proof that they are as human and as fallible as the rest of us, and are subjects for entertaining gossip. Even the most pious old ladies who tolerate no word of criticism against the

Church can be brought to smile over the errant behavior of one of its professionals.

Clergymen come and go regularly through our studio and home. We have known all kinds. Long ago, we—and our children—lost all concern for their hieratic status or special sensibilities. They are numbered among our friends, to share food and drink with, to talk and argue with, to fight with, and, occasionally, to grow to love.

A letter from an unknown priest once took me deep into the southwest desert, the middle of nowhere, as far from civilization as one can possibly get in the United States. I found a crumbling adobe church and rectory sitting in a flat expanse of burning scrub and cacti. Near the back door of the residence, a frowzy blond housekeeper was sunning in an abbreviated swimsuit. She responded to my self-introduction with an indolent finger pointed to that part of the house where I just might find the good father.

He was tall and emaciated, one of the homeliest men I'd ever seen, not unlike the grotesques from Da Vinci's celebrated sketchbooks. Big featured and coarse, with flesh stretched tight over prominent bones, he moved like a jerky, erratic mechanism, like some monstrous stringed marionette manipulated by an invisible puppeteer. Almost immediately, he suggested we walk—under that broiling sun—while he described the work he'd like done at the church. Of course he had very little money, but he wanted to bring his parishioners something beautiful. When I asked what parishioners, where were they in this (excuse me) God-forsaken inferno, he explained that they lived in hovels scattered for miles through the desert. They were mostly wetbacks and vagrants, outlaws to both American and Mexican immigration officials. They were people of God and needed something of beauty in their church, in their lives.

During subsequent months, I visited the lonely outpost whenever possible. The priest and I contracted work, and it went well. All of our business was discussed on tramps across the desert, Father's head capped with a knotted kerchief, his face seared lobster-red. In the flaming eyes, long nose, and full mouth, I saw more than obvious sensuality. I saw torments and old wounds that he carried from grievous suffering through war in Europe; and—often—radiance, a loving faith in Christ and man that transfigured his homeliness to beauty.

Early in the game, I perceived that he was mad but valued him for it. No sane person I had ever known tolerated such poverty and privation in the service of others. I met some of his parishioners and recognized that his work wasn't totally quixotic but was effecting hopeful change in a despised people.

I knew the chancery had driven him into the wilderness, where he wouldn't cause the institution embarrassment; but I saw him turning exile into opportunity, the chance to work toward grace. Whatever I thought about the sullen housekeeper and her suspicious breath was best left unspoken. Once, Father apologized for her rudeness, saying she was adrift, alone and unhappy, and had nowhere to go. Like the outlaws who entered his chapel knowing all these things and suspecting worse, I came to love this sinner. He was a good man.

The last time I visited the rectory, the housekeeper, dressed in a flimsy nightgown and reeking of whiskey, met me at the door with hysterical tears. Father was dying of cancer and had been taken to a hospital many miles distant. Abandoning schedules and all business, I sped across the fiery landscape, trying to outrace death. I had to see this exceptional human being, this Christian maverick, once more before he died. But the head nurse, a nun, greeted my alarm with open contempt. "Who told you he's dying? And he shouldn't have visitors, but you just go see for yourself."

He was propped up in bed, extremely weak, and drained of all the color I had known in his usually florid face. He had fallen off the wagon that I had always assumed he tortuously rode. He had been on a fearsome binge, was being dried out, and faced surgery. Did drugs make him so unusually talkative? There was an ironic reversal of priest-penitent roles, and I couldn't stop his compulsive flow of confessions. The stern nurse eventually came and asked me to leave.

He is rarely mentioned among mutual friends, and we never see him. Is he still, I wonder, in a sanitarium; and if so, where on God's green (or parched) earth will those destitute wetbacks find another selfless one like him? I occasionally hear him remembered in criticism as reprobate and sinner by a few sanctimonious brothers of the priesthood. But he gave me, I think, just a glimpse into the tough and true nature of sainthood.

I RECENTLY RODE Amtrak's Metroliner between New York and Washington, D.C. The sleek train covers those two hundred twenty-seven miles in three hours. Business is up and has established serious competition to air and bus services on this east-coast run. Reservations must be booked well in advance, and for the first time in more than twenty years there is hope that rail passenger service won't soon die out. A promotion brochure that I pick up in the snack-bar speaks of a vast untapped market—the ninety-six percent of Americans aged eighteen and over who have never ridden a train.

My father was a railroad man. I rode trains from infancy, and remembrance of that early experience of the rails has never left me. I knew the sights and sounds, the smell and touch of most of the great trains in the United States—and a few in Europe—and was at home in the famous terminals. After years of travel by jet plane and plenty of familiarity with international airports, my senses are not entirely free of railroad soot and smoke, chugging engines and clacketing cars, the long mournful moans of whistles through the night. The train, unlike the plane, never meant speed or anxiety about getting from one point to another in the least possible time. It meant settling down, usually alone, to hours or days of one's broken routine—a rare time, because of the cradling rhythm of the rails, for quiet thought and introspection. How many hundreds of faces I've glimpsed at train windows as their coaches glided slowly by mine in darkened depots; nearly always they were faces of people lost in thought, staring into the night.

The Metroliner is posh and comfortable. I close my eyes and surrender. Dozing on trains is a familiar pleasure; I drift in and out of short naps with practiced ease. But unsuspected fatigue begins to take its claim; I feel myself spiraling into the yawning chasm of deep sleep.

The rhythm has changed. It is no longer smooth, fast and modern, but broken by fits and starts. The day has given way to night. I see twisted metal and rubble through a small ragged hole that has replaced a picture window. We are stalled on a siding, and someone has thrown wide the sliding door of our boxcar. The moon is shining on a devastated landscape, illuminating a distant city of hollow walls, their shattered windows glowing like dead eyes against the frosty sky.

We have been jammed in these quarters for more days than any of us can remember. Unwashed, ill-fed, lice-ridden, we keep to the wooden bunks lining each wall; or occasionally, if we are cold, we hug the iron stove squatting in the center of the car. Foul moods and short tempers have driven us to insulation, each man instinctively holing up on his own narrow bunk, avoiding personal touch and conflict. At the frequent stops and delays, we seek outdoors and fresh air, and pace beside this troop train, which is incredibly long, seeming to us—in our madness—to have neither beginning nor end. We no longer know where we are, having criss-crossed national frontiers countless times in this zig-zag maneuver of an incomprehensible journey.

But someone is speaking German, explaining we are west of the Rhine and that this line—she knows it well—goes into Aachen.

Won't we give her and her teenaged daughter a lift? They know the country, are agile, and have had experience jumping from moving trains. They have family in Aachen, and must get off there. Beyond Aachen, the train rolls into France and they'd be in enemy hands. Brave young Americans help them on board and slam shut the door as the train begins to move.

A few of us seek the shelter of our bunks, but most of the men have crowded around the women. A strange game begins, Saturday afternoon on the gridirons of America, only this time the footballs are a middle-aged hausfrau and her daughter. Thrown and pummelled from one end of the jolting car to another, forward and back-passed, tossed into the air, the women scream alien words none of us wants to understand. Their terrified faces, hideously distorted by firelight, sail by like bizarre images from Hieronymus Bosch. Those men who disapprove try to shut out sight and sound, leaving the revel to barbarians who've ruled this car from the beginning. It is only when the women, bruised and bloodied, are thrown off the swiftly moving train—not at Aachen but within the enemy lines they feared—that the obscene laughs, shrieks, and howls subside. All men seek their own corners, locked in private anguish, watching the red glow of the stove. I hear a timid boy cry.

Bedlam again during a stop in a freightyard harboring shipments of wine. Casks are appropriated and hauled aboard the train, are broken open and emptied into canteens, helmets, and buckets. The bacchanalia continues as the train once again takes up its bleak passage—men come and go through the door now left open, crawl along the sides of the speeding train, fist-fight on tops of cars. Intoxicated warriors crash into red-hot stoves or lie unconscious in pools of sickness. We are delayed still again, briefly, beside a trainload of refugees on an adjacent track. For one endless moment, I stare into their starved, ravaged faces—a frieze of Semitic pain at this orgiastic misuse of wine.

It is dawn when some of us wake to see a young corporal standing in the open doorway. Someone shouts at him to relieve himself quickly and close the door, it's too damn cold. But the boy remains poised against the warming sky, bare trees careening drunkenly beyond his silhouette. Another man yells that he close the door. We watch the boy shrug his shoulders in total resignation, then leap deliberately into the void. We shall never see or hear of him again, and he will be an official statistic, Missing in Action.

The hand on my arm is the conductor's, nudging me to wakefulness. I look into his face, full and jovial, a well-trained representative for the crack Metroliner. Another trainman's voice, smoothly modulated over music-to-ride-trains-by, is heard from a concealed speaker-system, trusting we've enjoyed a pleasant morning and hoping we'll use Amtrak again in the future. The train has eased to a gentle stop, and a sane, orderly exodus is under way.

FEBRUARY

. . . the halt and the lame,
the diseased, maimed, deaf, and blind . . .

FEBRUARY days when the temperature climbs, we spend the noon hour in the garden, pruning, getting a headstart on the spring cleanup. The sheltering walls of the patio ward off chill winds, the sun gets trapped between house and stake fence, isolated patches of melting snow and ice send fingers of moisture over bricks and flowerbeds. Birds chatter at us from the highest branches of trees.

Amazing things are already happening on the surface of the earth. From atop a ladder over the grape arbor, I look down on Daria squatting near the green shoots of crocus and Kaufmania tulips. She pushes aside leafmold, uncovering more and more of the wakening plants. She raises her joyous face toward me, reporting each new discovery, each new "pink nose cracking the ground." Mara sits close to her, her huge paws beside the child's feet, her head cocked and ears tall at this latest experience—gardening—of puppyhood. Matassa the cat studies us all from a perch atop the wall. It is one of the better hours of the day in one of the finer times of the year, this noontime break under the winter sun, anticipating spring.

The vines are dense, and pruning goes slowly. I cut away old growth with extreme care, mindful of which leaders will be necessary for arbor shade as well as bountiful fruit. The main trunks are gnarled and toughened now, thickening into trees, dark and scarred against the fragile, tender offshoots of last year's growth. I smile at the obvious symbolism as I see Daria's fresh, eager face through the tangle of branches.

A few bunches of dried grapes, overlooked in the October harvest, tumble to the ground. I descend the ladder to move it farther down the arbor. How gratifying to look up and see that the work has progressed, that the sky has been opened wide with the cutting away of dead wood; and to think ahead toward June when the fresh and tender new leaves will bestow welcome shade; and bless us with food as Ellen prepares her traditional feast of dolmadakia, stuffed vine leaves. Beyond that, grapes on the table, wine in the cellar. Santa Fe remains many things to me; high on the list must be its receptivity to the cultivation of grapes.

Mara has leaped up, a swish of her strong tail knocking Daria off balance. The child cries and comes running to my arms. Kneeling on the bricked terrace, holding her, I hear the sobs cease and wait for her to return to the fascinating bulbs. But she is obviously tired and has no inclination to move. Head against my shoulder, eyes closed, she stands motionless, resting, savoring a still and quiet moment in her very active day.

It was so like this, so very long ago, with Immaculata. February, too, and under an orchard, and Immaculata had put a finger to her lips as well as mine, silencing all words. She closed her eyes and rested a white-haired head against my shoulder. It was her way of saying farewell, *addio, ti stringo al cuore*—I press you to my heart. I've never known how long we remained standing like that, but I often feel it was for eternity.

We had known each other less than two weeks, and on this day she had joined a procession of villagers escorting me to the train and my journey out of their lives. She was of my parents' generation and shared none of the mischief and torments of mine, but from our first meeting, at first sight, we recognized an extraordinary kinship of spirit. Meta de Sorrento had given me in brief, crowded days new adventures, indelible memories, a host of friends, and a family of previously unknown, lost, or obscure relatives. At the core of this kaleidoscopic experience was Immaculata, tall and stout, handsome, a woman of great beauty and strength, whom not only husband and children but half the town acknowledged as their heart. She was an amazing human being, in love with man and his universe, embracing pain and joy with equal fervor, her large arms open to anyone needing comfort, her laughter a gift to all, the ample bosom a pillow for all the tears of wearied man. I was flattered, and humbled, not only by the care she gave me, but by the quickness with which she offered her confidence and enlisted my aid in her voluntary ministry to others.

She took my hand and drew me away from the procession through a break in a wall into the orchard. Time stopped—or traveled backwards—as we stood together, her head on my shoulder; for this tower of strength, this mature and forceful woman, became again a small child, hurt, quietly grieving, surrendering once more someone she'd grown to love. I was intensely aware of all our surroundings, nature witnessing the silent ritual—winter sunlight dappling the trees, the fragrance of ripening oranges overhead, an idyllic blue sky, the sound of the Mediterranean far below. But I do not remember how or when I rejoined the procession, alone, while Immaculata remained in the grove and let others escort me to the train.

A TOURIST in our shop, disappointed that we do not carry conventional mass-produced items, says she has been looking for a small reproduction of Michelangelo's *Pietà*. Too bluntly, perhaps, I tell her that no acceptable commercial copies exist, that I've seen hundreds and that they're all bad. She replies that if one can't live in Rome, copies, good or bad, will have to do.

A second *Pietà*, or Deposition from the Cross, much less known, was executed by the great Renaissance artist near the end of his long life. It is housed in a dark alcove of the Duomo at Florence, and I prefer it to the more celebrated one in Rome. While a student at the Accademia, I visited the Duomo at least once every day for nearly a year and usually stopped before the *Pietà*. It is a large work, unpolished, its surface rough with the sure, masterful strokes of hammer and chisel. Christ rests limply between the arms of the two Marys, while behind Him, cradling the sagging body, towers an image of Nicodemus. Michelangelo used himself—old, battered, infinitely sad—as a model for the likeness of Nicodemus.

Modern Florentines are notoriously unsentimental about the great artists who built their city, and about many of the public works to be seen in convento, piazza, or palazzo. The foreigner's praise for a Lippo-Lippi madonna may be brushed aside with a bawdy rundown on the painter's scandalous behavior with his models; mention of Bandinelli invariably calls attention to his awkward statue of Giovanni delle Bande Nere—butt of many local rude jokes—which fronts the superb church of San Lorenzo and the Medici chapel. The Florentines' favorite monuments are often small and easily overlooked by casual tourists. The bronze boar in the straw market is beloved by all citizens; most appreciate the delicate grace of Verrocchio's diminutive winged boy in the courtyard of Palazzo Vecchio; and the Pitti Gardens' fat debaucher squatting astride a turtle is esteemed for its blatant rough-humored insolence.

I lived in Florence in a *pensione* run by two elderly sisters. Uneducated but shrewd, they took every opportunity to set foreign art-students straight about the city's riches. They would argue by the hour the failures of Gozzoli, Giambologna, Cellini, and Vasari while defending obscure, anonymous little fountains scattered throughout the narrow streets and wide piazzas. They delighted in the playfulness of many of these fountains, instructing me to observe the cleverness, wit, and practicality in the placement of vents. They attacked a Leonardo canvas but praised the door-knocker on a palace I'd never heard of, downgraded a Donatello I'd admired but rhapsodized over a carved end-panel of a church pew in a neighborhood where foreigners never ventured. After a while, indulging their perversity, I stopped expressing enthusiasm about the old masters and would jokingly goad the sisters into another ferocious tirade against one of the city's more revered landmarks.

But my comeuppance came one day after a deliberate, flippant reference to Michelangelo's *David*, which stands in the Accademia and under which I elbowed to class each day through hordes of tourists. "The slingshooter must be the most overrated piece of marble in all Italy," I said. The ladies received my remark in openmouthed alarm. And when they'd recovered from the shock, they retaliated with every fighting gesture, evil eye, and *maledizione* they knew.

"Not the Buonarotti!" they shouted. "No one speaks of him so disrespectfully." They pummeled me with torrents of words on the great man's honesty, simplicity, and integrity, on his freedom from corruption and from the decadence of Renaissance society, his love of common man, and his denial of the slick commercialism so prevalent among his peers painting and sculpting for church and state. If I didn't retract my words, they wanted me out of their house, out of Florence and Tuscany, in Calabria or the Abruzzi, away from "we Fiorentini" and out anywhere with "all those others," the barbarians.

Even as I backed off from their splendid fury, I realized that these two screeching harridans, illiterate, were giving me a truer insight into Michelangelo and the power of his work than any of my illustrious professors had been able to do. I not only apologized but arranged an outing to Casa Buonarotti, where scores of the lesser-known works of Michelangelo rest. The ladies had a contempt for museums—art belonged in the piazzas or churches, so everyone could see it—but they acknowledged my good intent.

I have rarely joked about art since, and never about Michelangelo.

THE YOUNG WOMAN stands timidly before me, asking the same questions, hesitantly, that so many of her generation have brought to our studio. Should she major in art at school; how can she know if her talent is big enough; can I recommend teachers and schools? She's not exactly sure that art is what she wants, but then she's not certain about anything—isn't art worth a try? Family and friends have tried to dissuade her, saying the profession is impractical and difficult. Is it, really, that difficult?

"It's horrendous!" the Maestro exploded. "Run, don't walk, out of the world of art. Escape, flee, be anything but an artist. Every other way of life is preferable. Go find one of them!" It was his standard greeting to new students, and served a clever purpose. He invariably lost half the enrollment on the first day. "Now that we've weeded out the cowards," he would announce to a diminished class on the second morning, "I intend to hound the unresolved from these studios. Within a week, I'll have under my instruction only those madmen compelled to remain here. If art is not compulsive with you—no whim, no hobby, no indecisive action; if you're still free to take it or leave it— leave it, vacate my studio now before I smell you out." By the third morning, our numbers had dwindled still further.

I was one of the Maestro's madmen for nearly a year. We worked in frigid rooms over the Piazza San Marco, bundled heavily against the cold, with models warmly pink on sides turned toward the wood-burning central stove, blue on sides facing away. We were cheerless and industrious, and almost noncommunicative. The few survivors from the original registration were of various nationalities, speaking different languages, few knowing Italian, which the Maestro employed in a manner I'd never heard elsewhere. Actually, he rarely spoke at all once his opening roars had reduced the class to manageable size. He growled or he swore; he flayed the air with his arms or indelicately affected retching before our canvases. The rare word of approval was a reluctant grunt. After a while, he seldom came to the studio, leaving routine procedures to an assistant, dropping in once a week or so for a quick glance at our work and indicating for the most part disapproval. Much of his time, we heard, was spent in the wineshops.

I stumbled upon him one day in a cellar café down an alley near the Uffizzi. He was hunched over an enormous plate of *trippa fiorentina*, with a generous *fiasco* of chianti at one elbow and a dozen cats brushing his legs, waiting for morsels he occasionally tossed to the stone floor. I tried to avoid him and hurriedly leave, but he boomed my name and ordered me to sit opposite him. "You've learned my language well, young fool," he said. "Now listen to it." And so I did, without a single interruption, for over an hour, until he pushed aside the empty plate and bottle and staggered into the Florentine sunshine.

"It's damned you are, *caro bambino,*" he said, "hopelessly, to the arts. Perhaps even more so than the other madmen who remain with me. Well, then, prepare for the worst. Grow a thick hide, rid yourself of romanticism, shed baby fat, steel yourself against a hell on earth worse than anything friend Dante, mooning over Beatrice, ever imagined. Renounce—now!—every luxury, leisure, love, and friendship, all the human comforts; embrace work, fatigue, despair, the constant goading of body and mind to their extremes, the common torments known to every man magnified a thousandfold in your miserable, seething, writhing bones and brain. Live a lifetime like that; and for it, accomplish the tiniest fraction of what you set out to do.

"You think success is sweet? I'm Internationally Famous, and it's all sour. The critics don't know what they're talking about, the public even less. And everybody resents success. Your closest loved ones stand by you through adversity and obscurity; but only let your work gain recognition, a bit of acclaim, and they, too, begin to despise you. *La comedia* is never *finita*. Run, *Imbecille*, maybe there's still time—into the arms of commerce or law or medicine, into a factory or to a farm, into something prosaic and safe and easy. If you possibly can, *fratello mio,* turn your back on all the arts and bolt for your life!''

The young woman is searching my face, still waiting for an answer to her question—"Is it, really, that difficult?" She is too tender, too soft and sweet; I cannot reply, and stand speechless before her. But she has looked deep into my eyes and seen there some pale reflection of the Maestro, and turns away in distress. I watch her go silently out the door into the snow.

WE HAD BEEN at Biarritz little more than a month when Joe proposed the trip to Lourdes. He had made enquiries, and, yes, trains were running, not precisely scheduled perhaps, but the French government was cooperating with the resident American university to offer weekend excursions to nearby historic points of interest.

Joe was majoring in business administration, and his classes, unlike mine in the arts, seemed to provide him little pleasure. He fretted that soldiering had made him unfit, undisciplined, for academic study, and that he'd never now, here or stateside, earn the degree his parents expected of him. He had remained shuttered in quarters at the Hotel Eugenie, agonizing over term papers and exams, while I drifted from painting and sculpture studios at the Villa La Rochefoucauld into the sunny squares and sidewalk cafés, onto the *plage* and the golden sands fronting the Miramar. Biarritz for me, though we were still uniformed and subject to military rules, was paradise after hell. I hadn't for one moment considered excursions out of Eden. But when Joe suggested Lourdes (he had to get away, and everyone should see the shrine), I immediately agreed to go with him.

We were one of the original odd couples. Disparate personalities, Joe and I were drawn together at the army university in southern

France because we had shared a common nightmare in central Europe. But we shared little else, differing in taste, habits, philosophy, and interests. We tolerated each other with reasonable good humor, and the frequent arguments were loud but never vindictive. My chief cause of annoyance with Joe was his priggishness, or prudery, a sense of propriety that two years of combat hadn't quelled. He was constantly being shocked—by language, by drinking, by wenching and blasphemy. I had seen him finger his beads at what many of us considered innocent, if outrageously hilarious, barracks talk. And on the train to Lourdes with him, noting that he crossed himself or muttered ejaculations each time we rounded a mountain curve or chugged over a lofty trestle, I began to fear that we were on a pilgrimage, not a tour.

That question surfaced soon after our arrival at Lourdes. If Joe brought to the shrine a troublesome superstition and a simplistic obeisance to the legalistic church he had accepted in childhood, I arrived barren to mysticism, majestically, condescendingly tolerant of whatever ways man devised to survive. Angry that I would not accompany him on an itinerary of devotions, Joe demanded to know why I'd come at all.

"Because I am curious."

We went separate ways, Joe to join the sparse group of pilgrims (travel was not general so soon after hostilities), I to loiter on their fringe. I visited the basilica and grotto, and tried very hard to concentrate on Bernadette Soubirous and her visions. The winter sun was warm, and under it the halt and the lame, the diseased, maimed, deaf, and blind lay on stretchers, sat in wheelchairs, or were carried to the wide area before the modest grotto. There were many uniformed Frenchmen among them. I studied testimonials and photographic exhibits at the nearby hospital, scrupulously refusing to accept or deny the claims of miraculous cures. And in the end I went outside the gates of the shrine to neighboring streets, where vendors hawked souvenir trinkets, particularly many-sized and -shaped glass vials to hold the restorative waters. I purchased a number of these to carry home, whenever and wherever that might be, to family and friends still living in the grace of faith.

Joe and I shared a compartment on the train back toward Biarritz. We had been comrades a long time, and differences at the shrine were put aside as we spoke of old campaigns and buddies back on the Rhine. Joe drank a bit of *vin rouge* I had brought along, and was unusually reflective. There was a serenity about him that I'd never before noticed. It induced in me an acute sense of emptiness.

The train stopped at Pau, with a conductor shouting that there'd be an unscheduled four-hour holdover. Joe and I went into the streets, where some kind of military commemoration was under way. Bands played, tricolors flew, veterans marched, and speeches were made. We went into a crowded café, where we could find room at a table only by squeezing onto a long bench against the back wall. My order for *pastis*, and my obvious appreciation of it once it arrived, brought a beam to the face of the elderly gentleman beside me. "Not many Americans order that!"

He had a ruddy, weatherbeaten face punctuated with lively eyes and capped by a jaunty beret. He had heard about the mobilization of Biarritz as a university center, and wanted to know if students were booked solidly into the grand hotels, if the cafés and shops were thriving, how long the United States could be expected to pump dollars into the fashionable resort. Joe tried a few times to speak of regional heritage, particularly of Lourdes. "Oh, yes, I've been there," the man commented pleasantly, then spoke immediately again of the thriving market on the coast.

Some of the marchers, singing the Marseillaise, entered the café. We all rose to our feet, the old man with great difficulty. Only then was I aware that his body was badly deformed, the spine twisted and crooked, his legs bent and turned inward. All through the long singing of the stirring anthem, I could not discipline myself to look away from his affliction. Nor cease to think of Lourdes and its promise of miracles so few miles away. The Frenchman grinned at me, at my youth, inexperience, and confusion. As soon as the song stopped and we were seated again, he offered a brief explanation. "Of course I went to the Madonna—many times, always with frustration, bitterness, and grief. But there are all kinds of lameness and all kinds of cures, *mon ami*. I am no longer crippled in the mind or in the soul. And that's a miracle I didn't know I was seeking until it was granted."

Then he turned to Joe and spoke again of commerce.

MARCH

. . . she lived out her life in a
continuous ministry to all who wanted or needed help . . .

ONCE in many years—and it's just happened again—putting the wrong pressure on one of my steel files will snap it in two. I look with disbelief at the studio table where the broken rasp lies beside the fragile plaster mold that destroyed it. How ironic that while I worked with tempered steel against the soft mixture of lime and sand, I was thinking of Maman.

She was physically delicate, thin and not very tall, fine boned and small featured. The one exception in this frail physiognomy were eyes overly large and black, luminous, ringed by deep sockets and high cheekbones. Even before I met her, observing her shopping or on errands in the streets of *la ville haute,* I suspected this outer shell was deceptive. Here was a woman of strength! She strode the cobbled lanes of her Belgian village ramrod straight, head high, with purpose. And she had flair. Though always dressed in mourning black, she was partial to capes, shawls, and wimples, which lent her a delightful, theatrical air of mystery.

I was brought to her home by a comrade who had seen Maman's daughter in the town square and was bold enough—fortified with cognac—to bang on their door one night. He had the besotted notion that both women would welcome conquering heroes with open arms. Maman's arms were at her sides as she stood in the doorway and harshly demanded our business; and one hand was concealed under an apron.

Her judgment of us was swift and firm. My coarse companion was to go away, but I was welcome to share the *caffee latte* she was brewing. I followed her through a dark hall to the kitchen and watched her take the pistol, a Luger, from under her apron before reaching for the coffee cups.

She lived behind drawn blinds and locked doors, caring for daughter and grandchild while husband and son-in-law languished in foreign prison-camps. Maman was born (ordained) to care for others, a seasoned pro at recognizing need and moving to meet it. She had lost her husband to the tortures of political imprisonment, because together they had befriended, housed, and nursed wounded Allied parachutists. Her parlor was constantly visited by desperate friends and relatives wanting money or food handouts, counsel, release from fear. I grew accustomed to the sight of her cradling young and old, male or female, in her slender arms, murmuring comfort. More than from the coins or scraps of bread she managed to release from meager reserves, they drew strength from her cool presence and quiet words. Over and over I heard it whispered to sobbing faces: "Courage, courage, courage."

She was visited, too, by antagonists, local townspeople whose national loyalties differed from hers, and who came to warn her about aiding questionable refugees. Military from three nations had commandeered her home at various times, and acts of mercy had falsely branded her an "enemy collaborator." The Luger was picked up each time the doorbell rang.

I was welcome as a son, she said. And she initially offered maternal interest in my material comforts—hot meals, laundry, sewing and mending chores. But we were locked in too deep an understanding of each other for such a superficial relationship to endure. We were fighters for survival, using everything and everyone to keep body and soul intact. I hungered for people and interests other than my rude comrades and our brutal occupation; Maman wanted a trusted man in the house, even with his rough humors and language, someone to bolster, no matter how temporarily, her heavy responsibility of sheltering daughter and grandchild against the daily horrors of a world gone mad.

We escaped into music and song, played on a battered piano and sung badly but with gusto. We retrieved champagne from cellar caches, feasted on gourmet dishes prepared from the unlikely tins of appropriated military supplies. I brought responsible friends to the house, skits were improvised, long evenings of story-telling drowned out overhead bombers. Maman proved an innate thespian, acting out for us the highlights of her life on tabletop or against the proscenium of kitchen walls. It was wholesale catharsis, there in those small rooms every night of the week for anyone admitted to the house. When I saw laughter, finally, in Maman's daughter, a young woman emotionally broken by a shelling that had trapped her under a dead soldier, I believed a miracle had taken place.

"And perhaps it has," Maman said, "but I forbid you to speak anything provocative to the others. You and I go on leading the song and dance."

Only once, when she had had a drop too much champagne, did Maman desert the ship's bridge. She was drifting into sleep on a sofa, and friends and I gayly made a ritual of covering her with blankets. As the others respectfully moved off, she took my hand and I saw tears in her eyes. "Forgive my taking too much wine, Andre. But I'm so tired of being strong, so afraid I can't be much longer. My husband used to say that the weak feed on the strong, and that they'll destroy me."

But the steel in Maman never snapped like the broken file I hold in my hands. Nor did it roughen her delicate beauty, soft as the smooth plaster mold I touch. And the weak did not destroy her. Rather, she lived out her life in a continuous ministry to all who wanted or needed help, growing stronger and stronger in the love of others as she stripped away all concern for self.

THE ARCHITECT spreads the drawings wide on a table before us. We've been working closely with him for some months on the concept and design of a church renovation. His visits to Santa Fe result in conferences stimulated by the transformation of perceptual ideas into graphically realized plans and elevations. The collaboration on the project, though construction is not yet under way, has already resulted in a personal relationship far beyond professional requirements and demands. Into the building is going much that he is and we are; and discussion of any design problem exposes basic tenets of taste, judgment, and sensibility—inevitably, of philosophy and faith.

Designing churches is an intimidating business. The designer and associate artists are usually involved not with a single client but with clergy, building committees, liturgical commissions, occasionally with hefty segments of a large congregation, many of them quite convinced that their ideas about sacred space are as valid as those of any professional. Meetings and discussions, frequently as heated as in any other forum, can be debilitatingly complicated by impractical, visionary, or tenuous proposals emerging from the sincere desire to establish—modest or grand—a spiritual, as well as temporal, house of the Lord. Passions can flare violently over disagreements as slight as the placement of candlesticks. Permanent feuds can develop over the arrangement of furnishings in a sanctuary. God knows, and history has proven, that one helluva lot of mischief is done in the name of the Lord.

Early in our career, we believed with other neophytes to the liturgical arts that the trade would somehow grant us a miraculous dispensation from human folly. In naïve astonishment, we discovered that architects, artists, building committees and, yes, princes of the Church, remained stubbornly mortal, sloshing through the mud of mankind's frailty while reaching for the stars. We had difficulty reconciling conscientious and laborious attempts to express the sublime in an edifice, with the petty peccadillos that persisted throughout its construction.

Inspired by the vision and reverence that many individuals brought to such projects, we were at the same time disillusioned when pride, greed, jealousies, and vindictiveness mounted even as the walls of the temple rose higher against the sky.

I remember self-righteously discussing my confusions one evening among a group of seasoned veterans in the liturgical arts, with whom I was sharing a rectory's cache of Irish whiskey. My colleagues had all long since abandoned the illusion that their work, any more than the truth, would set them free—from their transgressions, anyway. The point was simply to go on striving, to wrestle each day the profanities in themselves as zealously as they struggled with the perverse complexities of design and building.

"It's never been otherwise," a man twice my age remarked. "Do you think that Chartres, the Sistine Ceiling, Santa Sophia, or St. Peter's was built by anyone less than the angels? Under the scaffolds of those magnificent structures, within the shadows of their glorious mosaics and frescoes, the artisans and workmen lived—and sinned—for years. No transfiguration abruptly curtailed their heritage from Adam. The victory of art is that it permits man to express his divinity while remaining subject in his mortality to all the ills and torments of the mind, the soul, and the flesh."

Our labors were easier after that. But the wise gentleman did not have the definitive answer, as no one has or will have, about the mystique of successful religious architecture and art. He spoke from a Christian bias, yet I have felt that same pervasive certainty of man before his gods in the ruins of the Acropolis and the Forum, at the pyramids of Teotihuacan, in the modest adobe kivas, and in the structured sand-paintings of Indians of the American Southwest. I have seen it in small bowls fashioned from clay, as well as in the loftiest, many-spired cathedrals of Western man.

If it is humbling, liturgical art is also a proud profession, affording its tradesmen the luxury of service to others and tolerating (over time) little that is false. Its disciplines can free a man from enervating selfness, forcing him to forsake indulgence in isolationist, therapeutic art, compelling him to reach out toward his brothers. His survival in the profession depends ultimately on his success at touching others.

Noting the architect's patient, hundredth revision of a detailed drawing; admiring Ellen's sensitive solution to the contours of a critical, sculptured wall; studying the honest craftsmanship of contributing associates from Italy and New Mexico; speaking with concerned priest-client or members of his building committee, I know that we are embarked on a grand and glorious adventure—to tear from ourselves the best that is in us, to uncover strengths and talents that only this particular challenge can liberate. And to do so within our own immense limitations, despite doubts, fear, fatigue, and whatever mischief we engender along the way. We shall probably become much more vocal about immediate, practical problems of the project, than about its aesthetics. For liturgical artists are constantly threatened, even more so than secular artists, by corruption of good work through nonproductive, theoretical shoptalk. The danger of pietism is ever present, and all concerned must frequently remind themselves that temples to the Lord are built by sinners.

REPRODUCTIONS of paintings on the passion, death, and resurrection of Christ have come under my eye constantly during the past few weeks. Requested by a Lutheran Synod to produce an audio-visual presentation on the Lent and Easter theme, I've been examining hundreds of 35mm slides from museums and collections the world over. Many of the pictures are old friends; some are new, exciting discoveries. In all are manifest the wonders of individuality and creativity that countless artists have persistently brought to this subject from the first century A.D. until today.

A painting by Giottino (*c.* 1350) is an especially welcome re-acquaintance. It is thought the artist never received personal instruction from the master Giotto, but was profoundly influenced by him. Giottino's "Deposition" is an intriguing reconstruction of Giotto's favorite subject-matter, exquisitely colored and of great sensitivity.

I once enjoyed the Giottino with a close friend who suddenly appeared beside me in the Uffizzi and immediately exploded into a loud attack on most of that famed gallery's paintings—"not this one, of course. I'm quite delighted to find someone standing in front of it. The tourists never get farther than Botticelli and his Venus on the half-shell."

Cathy was an American from a ranch in the northern Rockies, a big woman with an enormous voice, studying under one of the finest singing-teachers in Europe. She was a genuine one-hundred-percent, dyed-in-the-wool eccentric, a creature of flamboyant dress and make-up, the grand dramatic flair and gesture. Intelligent and generous, with an acid wit, she had a large retinue of friends who not only tolerated but loved her outrageous costumes and behavior. I had, early in our friendship, been embarrassed when her huge presence, aided by theatrical makeup, turned heads our way in the streets of Florence.

But now I was accustomed to getting public notice when with Cathy. She paced furiously before the Giottino, her hands impatiently tossing about innumerable scarves attached somehow, somewhere, to her ample frame, her eyes flashing fire behind mascara as bold as Nefertiti's, her voice booming across the wide salon and echoing off the walls. I saw the gallery attendant respectfully keep his distance—few Florentines had not felt the wrath of La Signorina Grande del West.

She loved this painting (she said with anger) because it was one of the few Renaissance works on the Passion free of cant and sentimentality. I challenged this extravagant statement but got no retraction, merely a blaze fanned higher. After three years in Italy, she was tired of "the sensuality hiding behind religious themes, these erotic hedonists we're supposed to accept as saints because somebody put a halo around their heads. Give me pagan art where nobody's trying to fool anybody else about such things!"

Shouting in Italian—she always spoke the language of the country she happened to be in—she was running the risk of offending the national pride of Tuscans within earshot, and precipitating another of her frequent international incidents. I was relieved to see the tirade finally lose momentum, slow down, and gradually move, with brilliant staging, from presto furioso to adagio pianissimo.

Cathy respected art too much to touch the surface of a masterwork, but her elegantly gloved hand hovered perilously close to the Giottino. She was pointing out, *sotto voce,* the fact that all the figures in the composition—except that of the dead Christ—were frowning. "They're in grief, yes, but don't you feel they're puzzled and angered, too? How extraordinary of that little man to paint them that way— surely, it's a more human reaction than rolling eyes skyward and looking pious." She was especially captivated by the Magdalena, who, she said, looked "almost disgusted at what's happened on Calvary, and certainly abandoned. That's how I'd have felt."

The gallery attendant had mustered the courage to draw near, his eyes darting about in an attempt to monitor Cathy's fluttering hands. She scolded him mercilessly, reminding the unfortunate man that she'd never abuse anything in the Uffizi because she undoubtedly had a better understanding and appreciation of Florentine treasures than he. She followed with a discourse against all local citizens who, she said, were a "false aristocracy wallowing in self-righteousness! Give me, anytime, the self-proclaimed sinners like the Magdalena in the painting."

The attendant had begun to plead for restraint, but Cathy's attention was already elsewhere, at the end of the room, where a gentleman in impeccable dress stood in the doorway. He was her Italian "escort," whom she had introduced to me the week before, explaining such companions were "absolutely essential in this insanely sensuous country!"

Cathy met her own Calvary—illness, suffering, an early death— within a few years. The great fame predicted for her by every leading voice-critic in Europe was never realized. For a while, those of us who had loved her felt cheated and robbed, just as she said the figures in the Giottino painting did. But their expressions of confusion and grief are brushed in paint forever; ours have already vanished. We can rejoice in thoughts of Cathy, and be grateful for her generous spirit, which will continue to touch and enrich us for as long as we live. Such a transition from sorrow to joy is not unlike that which artists have always expressed in moving on from paintings of Golgotha to those of Easter morning.

ALL I CAN HEAR in the hushed chapel are flickering candles, burned low and nearly extinguished, sputtering against the mauve glass of vigil lights. It is late, and I should go home. But there's much to be done—Lent is once again with us, and I am committed to arts in the service of the church. I've been programming a short meditation, slides synchronized to music, for presentation at a Sunday liturgy. Tired, I sit and listen to a playback of the taped music: brief excerpt from a Vivaldi Mass, immediately followed, with surprising effectiveness, by an American spiritual sung by Marian Anderson.

Lights are low in Santa Fe's "media chapel," a pale blush of seasonal purple washing the sculptured walls, a few soft spotlights touching the Tabernacle and the fine, locally carved crucifix. It is good to be alone in this space that the parish community calls sacred. When the music ends, I am reluctant to return to work.

Multi-media is not exactly new to me. In addition to my work in graphic arts, I've always been involved with journalism, with amateur still-photography and movie-making, with peripheral aspects of radio and television, and with home recording. But multi-media's use in churches is new, and only in the past three years have I been seriously challenged to employ it along with more traditional liturgical arts. Though technical problems are totally different from those of painting and sculpture, multi-media demands many of the same principles and disciplines necessary for successful work in those arts.

Listening to replay after replay of the recorded music in a projection booth, I study banks of 35mm slides on illuminated viewers. The music has been chosen because it expresses the theme of a particular liturgy; and now I must select images that not only illustrate scriptural texts of that liturgy but are a visual complement to the sound. Slides of classical and modern art, contemporary scenes and landscapes, symbols, flora and fauna, the Sistine ceiling, and massacres in Indo-China march before my eyes.

Another hour passes, during which I'm oblivious to everything but the excitement of seeking whatever line, color, and form will best make visible the Word.

The work goes well. After a few run-throughs of the programmed meditation, I begin to shut down equipment. A knock on the closed door startles me, for I had thought the chapel was empty. Two young men, bearded itinerants, long locks of hair falling over their shoulder-packs, stand in the doorway and say they've watched the rehearsals projected on chapel walls, and are very moved. And curious. Dropouts from the Church (and society), they had no idea technology was being introduced into liturgy. Is this, perhaps, some underground community working against the institution? When I say that the parish is completely orthodox, pioneering new uses of the arts within established dogma, they look disappointed.

Anarchy is the only answer—to Church, government, to every outmoded cultural and social institution we've too long tolerated. They are sure that the "sensitive work you're doing must be widely misunderstood and attacked by the Establishment." Yes, and also by the anti-Establishment, for our insistence that renewal be rooted in the past has drawn fire from progressives, as well as reactionaries. And yet, the liturgies attract more and more people, many from great distances, who are looking for new ways that do not insist on abolishing an old and rich heritage.

The boys' eyes are luminous—not, I suspect, from youthful fervor, but from recent pulls on marijuana. They speak gently, barely above a whisper, of grievous loss, not only in the Church but everywhere. Without home or family, without other friends, without interests or employment, they are wandering the country not knowing what, if anything, they seek. When I say that all generations have experienced similar disillusionment, and that it's often a condition of youth, they smile indulgently at someone older who they assume has never been there. And they pull closer together, in physical contact against the world of elders. Inevitably, cursing my own capitulation to cultural slogans, I think Gay Liberation.

The boys have grown increasingly defensive, and I have to assure them that I have no quarrel with their personal ideologies. Half my age, without strong convictions, they fail repeatedly in weak attacks against my resolve to work for change within, not without, institutions. And they seem confused (perhaps even disappointed) by the fact that I don't try to force, father-fashion, my ideas on them. One accuses me of being harsh, "too pragmatic for the mystical," and the other asks why I don't proselytize. "Everybody does. People your age as well as the Jesus Freaks. We were with them on the coast, and they're from nowhere, just like everybody else."

It's midnight. The air has cleared, and I must close the chapel. The young men want to remain a few minutes longer while I do final chores. They sit quietly in the dim, silent chapel, staring at the carved crucifix. I fight the thought that they are behaving in an affected manner, acting, mimicking a religiosity I find intolerable in the professionally pious. But my work in the chapel permits no license for such judgments, and I concentrate on practical tasks.

At the door, we wish each other well. I am thinking how ill-prepared these soft young people are to face whatever the night and future hold. One stays my hand as I draw the door shut. He takes a last look into the chapel, bows his head and mutters. I think I hear him correctly: "Good night, sweet Prince."

AN EERIE STILLNESS lay over the casino. Lights were extinguished on all upper floors and on the staircase landings; doors that normally stood ajar day and night were now uniformly closed against deserted hallways. In the cavernous grand salon, stripped of nearly all furnishings except a massive pool table, one naked light bulb cast a feebly yellowish glow over the green field of sport. On the flat felt lay an opened issue of "Stars and Stripes," its inflammatory headlines shrieking of the massacre at Malmedy and the siege of Bastogne. In a far dark corner, a blanketed man slept soundly on a cot opened taut before his silent telephone switchboard. Beyond the salon's huge window-wall, moonlight touched the valley's fields of snow and glinted goldenly, prismatically, off the frozen surface of the Sambre.

Our sentry, abandoning his frigid post in the Rue Grande before the casino's doors, suddenly appeared at my side. Younger even than I, cold and frightened, he complained that a woman was in the street, against all security, violating curfew, and demanding to see me. She wouldn't go away, dammit, even though he'd repeated again and again that we were all restricted to quarters; and he didn't know what to do about her. I told him the whereabouts of some *vin rouge* concealed in my room, put on his overcoat, shouldered his M-1, and volunteered to walk his post for a short relief.

Phoebe was huddled against the side of the building, seeking shelter from icy winds careening down the narrow main street of the *ville haute*. She had Agnes with her, the small child almost hidden under her mother's threadbare coat, her sleepy eyes peering anxiously out at a dark, cold world.

"We've come to say adieu."

Of course they would know about the impending troop movement, no matter how severely Intelligence had cut us off from them. Civilians always knew, frequently before the troops were issued orders. The Belgiques had long practice at observing armies and interpreting actions outside locally appropriated billets. They were older veterans than any of us.

Phoebe could do little but weep. She made no attempt to check her tears, find brave words, or offer hope. "First Papa to the Boche, then my husband, now you who's become my brother." She didn't hear when I spoke of our risk at violating civilian curfew and military restriction, but stared at me out of eyes like those of a crazed casualty, helpless and without fight. I tried to make bad jokes—because inanities kept so many of us going—but Phoebe would not tolerate them. "How can you, you and Maman, escape in a glass of wine, a song and a dance, a vulgar story? How do you manage to put the truth aside?" No words I uttered had any meaning to her, but were empty phrases, platitudes about a survival she didn't want and couldn't believe in.

The little girl tentatively touched my hand; and when I'd kissed the child's uplifted face, Phoebe moved away from us into the center of the cobbled street. "Come, Agnes," she whispered. And to me, "I will send Maman."

Maman bore a gift, a heavy cardboard carton stuffed, she assured me, with breads, broiled rabbit, a little white wine, and some bottles of black beer. She bore, too, as always, the gift of herself, filling our brief minutes together with a controlled but passionate monologue. "My daughter says her farewell went badly. You must forgive her. She is very fragile—only I know how fragile—and there have been too many farewells. From what information we get through the Red Cross, her father has been broken physically, her husband, in spirit. And that information was so long ago, they could well have since died as prisoners. Now you go.

"We have loved you, *cher* André, as son and brother—and for me, the laughter which grew between us has been salvation. There'll be no one now—not Papa, not my son-in-law, not you—to share the wine, a meal, rough black humor and mischievous conversation. Never again your bawdy songs at the piano or my dance atop the table. No more this tender kinship between a foreign boy and a woman old enough to be his mother. No more furlough for either of us. Back to business. And what a monstrous business it is. Phoebe, somehow, endures through tears; I can only survive through laughter.

"For the future, I will hear nothing but your safety. I hope to hear it from you. But please tell your comrades that, tell them for me: Maman will hear nothing else!"

In the morning, she stood with daughter and granddaughter among the crowds in the Rue Grande who had come to watch our convoy prepare for departure. Snow was falling, the air was bitterly cold, but it seemed all the citizens of Thuin were assembled for our send-off. They were mostly strangers. Few alliances had been formed during our occupation, the civilians fearful of charges of collaboration by the Boche who might very well retake the town, the military ordered not to fraternize with an unknown, suspect populace. Maman and I had broken the rules at our very first encounter when we recognized that we could bring each other some degree of sanity in a landscape of the insane.

Maman was breaking rules again. Leaving Phoebe and Agnes among the still, silent ranks of onlooking townsfolk, she came forward to the open truck in which I sat and handed up an opened bottle of cognac. "It will keep you warm, *mon enfant*. Share it only with those who've been generous to you." She was smiling, refusing not to, refusing to be defeated by fear, anger, or grief. Ignitions roared; motors turned over in trucks, half-tracks, and weapons-carriers; officers shouted commands. Maman stood straight and proud among the traffic and confusion, relishing my first hearty swallow of the cognac. I was suddenly aware of how very small she was, *si petite*, short and lean, so delicate, really very beautiful, and not old. Just past forty?

Our truck lurched. Phoebe ran into the street and grabbed the tailgate. She stumbled along beside the vehicle as it gained momentum. The man beside me, an educated cynic, muttered hoarsely. "Melodrama. The Big Parade. Cinema." Phoebe was thrown to the ground. Just as we rounded a corner of the Rue Grande and before losing sight of them, I saw Maman move to her daughter's side and help her to her feet.

APRIL

He was on his knees
at the back of the great basilica,
oblivious to the crowds about him . . .

EACH DAY the child and I, hand in hand, walk the dog along the rito. We know well the paths, where the underbrush is thick, where the narrow stream-bed is most easily forded. The dog bounds to and from us, frequently maneuvering in wide circles, then charging at lightning speed, low to the ground, stopping only when she's beside the little girl—butting against her, cautiously nipping her ankles, forcing the child to give ground.

"There she goes again," Daria exclaims in feigned exasperation, pursing her lips and rolling her large round eyes heavenward.

"She's substituting you for a lamb," I try to explain. "Sheep dogs have the instinct to herd sheep, and Mara's only obeying a natural impulse."

"Why do they want to *hurt* sheep?" the four-year-old asks. My explanation continues.

The daily walks are instruction periods for myself, as well as for Daria and Mara. Certainly the overgrown, powerful puppy has much to learn. Her great strength and energy seem to preclude all thought as she crashes from one distraction to another. We watch her flush birds, tear like the wind through low grasses, plunge into thickets, run a length of the rito over slippery rocks and down small waterfalls. Occasionally she will meet a stray dog and usually tire him quickly with her undisciplined rough sport. Daria and I take turns calling com-

mands. The shepherd seems increasingly to understand but is not ready
to obey. She's a free soul who won't yet submit to reining in. Not
wanting to break her spirit, wanting her obedient and cooperative but
not cowered, I let the training go slowly as Mara enjoys the wild
chases. Of course she's intelligent, knowing full well to whom she
belongs, never letting us out of her sight and racing back to us at the
first real or imagined threat. Like the child in many ways, she is bold
and independent, a bit rebellious in defying authority but secure in the
family unit, scooting under its protective umbrella at the first clap of
thunder.

They seem light-years younger than I, bringing to these walks nothing clouded from their crowded day, living in the moment. We have
seen together the steady advance of spring, and Daria has forced me to
look with renewed interest at many of its timeless wonders. We've
watched the pussy-willow at water's edge swell and blossom and begin
to fade, noted the red blush of tamarisk and the first green leaves of
rampant elms. Weed and ground vines day by day push higher in the
paths we tread; here's a wild rose leafing out, and "why's that plant
called rabbit brush?" She has trouble with the word *chamisa* and lis-
tens patiently to my discourse on languages and indigenous plants. Ant
hills fascinate the child; she expresses the wish to pull one asunder and
see "what they're doing in there." Robins dart above and around us,
or splash in the small pools between sleek stones. When they chatter
and cavort in ritual flight, Daria is curious about their behavior. We
talk of courtship and nesting, eggs and fledglings. The little girl makes
me stop and peer with her into the trees. Babies, the young, are matters of consummate interest; already in the child I see that feminine
mystique that no male will ever fully comprehend.

The dog has stopped short, hackles raised. As we approach her, I
see a man nearby, lying on the river bank, unmindful of us or anything
else, an emptied bottle of cheap wine upended near his side. He looks
chilled, his legs drawn up tightly in the fetal position, his arms hug-

ging close a thin tattered shirt. Mara, who usually runs to strangers with enthusiasm, stands frozen, puzzled. As is Daria, who recognizes that this sleep is somehow different from what she knows, that it expresses pain. I feel her hand tighten on mine. Urging her and the dog to be quiet, I lead them slowly away, not without a sense of weariness, some acknowledgment that the beaten man lying shriveled in adobe dust was once as fleet as Mara, as wide-eyed and wonderstruck with his universe as Daria.

But we are in the open field now, both child and dog running on this final lap toward home. Technology and the media have had their way with me, for the mind is playing tricks with the eye, seeing girl and shepherd in an exquisite ballet of slow motion, freeze-framing their graceful leaps and pirouettes against a setting sun. When I catch up with them to leash Mara for the approach to traffic, Daria excitedly points to our nearby driveway and front terrace. Her tree—"my own, my very own tree"—has burst into bloom, and she wants to stand under the slender branches. It's a purple-leaf plum, presented to her by a grandmother and planted by parents while she was yet in the womb. She opens her arms wide as if she'd like to catch the blossoms swaying above her. Mara is beside her, head cocked in confusion, not understanding the source of pleasure. Beyond them, beyond the plum's glorious raiment, I see the glistening snows on the peaks of the Sangre de Cristo, melting now, lifting the rito, soon to course joyfully over the land, enriching us all.

THE MAESTRO was one of those maddeningly inexplicable Roman Catholics. I never knew a greater sinner, a man more susceptible to the temptations of the flesh, more obscene, blasphemous, quicker to damn orthodoxy and every professional in the Vatican. He had no use for formal prayer, was intolerant of conventional ritual, and wouldn't be caught dead among punctual communicants at a scheduled Mass. Vulgar gestures were his response to any suggestion that he formally, publicly acknowledge his Christian heritage in community action. "I know my Lord and He knows me," the Maestro would snarl at anyone daring to question his errant behavior.

More typical of the man, and familiar to his students at the Accademia, were his untempered passions, his insistence that we lavish our canvases with unrestrained libido, vomit in paint those festering fantasies, let it all flow. He burned.

Those of us who frequented the bars of Firenze also knew another Maestro—considerably less than invincible compared to the professor shielded by studio-classroom walls. The Maestro of the wineshops was a vulnerable man; and eternally, hopelessly snared in Catholicism.

I ran into him one Palm Sunday after most Florentines had preened themselves and ventured out to obligatory calls at the fashionable Duomo, Santa Croce, or Annunziata. The Maestro was firmly entrenched in a favored cellar off the teeming markets bordering San Lorenzo and the Medici Chapel. He growled at my arrival in the subterranean depths. And for a little while—the duration of my first two glasses of strong, unaged chianti—he turned his back to me. But we shared a terrible knowledge of each other; and in time, as I knew he would, he stood at my shoulder.

"*Cretino,*" he greeted me, "mightn't we just as well imbibe together?" I raised my glass in salute.

I listened politely to his dismal account of domestic woes, some sordid confessions of marital infidelities and insurmountable complications with his *affari d'amore.* It all seemed inconsequential, excusable. I knew his canvases, their exquisite sensitivity and the lie they gave his outrageous deportment. I knew, through his work, the man; no matter how he denied himself. And I had loved him since the first day we'd measured each other across the cold distance of the Accademia's bare studio. He had cursed me many times since; beyond the profanities was a concerned, painful, intolerable recognition that I could be, like him, nothing but an artist.

We emerged from the cellar long after midday. The piazzas were deserted; sensible Florentines were shuttered in siesta following the heavy Sunday dinners. The Maestro considered his family, awaiting him, but easily argued that away. Would I go with him to San Marco? I was such a poor student, so miserable a painter, and the *convento* would be reopening now—didn't I care to learn from a true master? Yes, we'd go to see the Fra Angelicos.

I had been there before—many times—and stood in awe, again and again, before the incredible frescos. How had the simple friar arrived at these basic shapes, that spare composition, dismissing everything superfluous, making his profoundly mystical statements with the greatest economy of line and form? How much study, training, discipline could produce similar results? Could any of us be taught, or learn, anything comparable—or was such facility a gift, a grace beyond all acquired technique, all scholarship? *Professore*, teacher, mad and dissolute but brilliant practitioner of the arts, can't you tell me?

He was beyond me. Standing before the luminous panel of *Gesu al Sepolcro*, my lusty Maestro was subdued, transfixed, abject. I tried a weak joke about the wine and its debilitating, sentimental effect. The Maestro motioned me silent. I persisted: if not the wine, what then in this masterful but formal composition moved him so? What did he see, what had I to learn? Tell me the secret, open the doors, Maestro, to the mysteries of great painting.

"*Imbecille*," he groaned. "*Americano—Stupido—Protestante!* Have you forgotten it's Palm Sunday, the first day of Holy Week? Do you think I'm looking only at a fresco? I am a Catholic, God help me, this day entering Jerusalem and this week climbing to Calvary. The painting at this moment is no more than an illustration to remind me of Gesu's passion. If we must be analytical," he struck his forehead, "it succeeds in that."

We had no school the remainder of that week; I did not see the Maestro at class. I sought him, against my will, in the wineshops, but without success. He continued to puzzle me, and I mentioned him to the *patrona* at the *pensione* where I lived. "*Dio mio!*" she exclaimed. "What a reprobate, what a *disgraziata* to the city. You mustn't think the people of Firenze are all libertines like him. The Accademia should dismiss him and not expose nice young foreigners like yourself to such poor ambassadors of Italia, such degenerates as he." She urged me, piously, to attend Holy Week services. And on Good Friday, not fully understanding why I was there, rationalizing to myself that it was to see, once more, the Michelangelo "Deposition," I entered the Duomo.

Caro, caro Maestro. He was on his knees at the back of the great basilica, oblivious to the crowds about him; oblivious, I suspected, to the formal liturgy; alone with his God on brutal, glorious Calvary; bent in agony under lash and nail and thorn—and transgressions. I put a hand upon his shoulder, but he never knew it. Great sinner, great believer. Moving toward the stone of Michelangelo—the sculptor's age and suffering carved into the likeness of Nicodemus—I pondered the strange, bewildering, enviable faith of Catholics; and Catholicism.

LATE STORMS this spring have coincided with the arrival of mail-order nursery stock at our house. I find the boxes marked "Perishable" sitting in inches of snow under the mailbox. Attached instructions guarantee that the perennials have been shipped "at proper planting time for your area" (but nobody understands New Mexico weather) and should go immediately into the ground. Ours this year have gone into the refrigerator while we await April thaws.

Quite a few seasons have passed when we have ignored the seductive seed and flower catalogues of January and ordered nothing. The gardens seem to have taken on their own character and resent too much interference. Well-established trees and shrubs, grapevines and roses flourish despite high-altitude extremes of coldness and warm sunshine; self-seeding, indigenous plants give us abundant bloom. No need to introduce anything more.

But one day I heard Daria speak of strawberries, and I realized she had never had the thrill of picking them fresh from the garden. Before she was born, we had sacrificed the small area reserved for berries. Older brothers and sisters, remembering the pleasure of raiding the patch before breakfast, had made her curious about what she had missed. I retrieved discarded nursery catalogues, and out went orders again.

One rare Saturday, when the persistent snows stopped falling and the sun blazed, Daria and I built a strawberry mound. I had read that pyramids of earth were a good solution to space restrictions for berry growing, and our original plan was for a tall, slender cone. But my earth-engineering collapsed midway through that, and we settled for the mound. It is located in an old outdoor firepit, rarely used since we've taken better thought of ecology and forfeited burning our trash. The molded earth is contained within wire-mesh, which we cut at intervals to make room to set the plants. I have an idea that once they green up, we're going to have a bizarre-looking ceremonial burial-mound smack in the middle of the patio.

Daria was out the next morning looking for strawberries. Even as I tried explaining to her the slow stages of growing, and recognized disappointment in her eyes, I could see the learning process underway. Here she was up against deferred pleasure, not the immediate gratification promised us—even the very young—by current bombardments of hard-sell media. She wanted to know when, after leaves and blossoms, she could expect berries. It was difficult to answer with weeks or months—time remains incomprehensible in her magical world. I remembered her birthday and said the berries would be ripe when she turned four in June. Daria's face lit with wonder, and she pressed her face against the damp soil. I was thinking of the commitment I had just made—how, if the mound does not thrive and produce fruit by June, I shall have to scatter store-bought berries there on that special morning.

They were wild strawberries growing in tangled clumps under an apple orchard. Wilhelmina's brows reflected their rosiness as she rooted in the thick runners, biting off fruit like a famished animal. Every once in a while, she raised her head to peer through the tree branches when the helicopter motors roared. The stupid thing was back again, circling the sky.

The helicopter contained military police scouring the countryside for criminals just like us. With guns recently silenced and the armies idled, the military sought many ways to busy itself. One was an attempt at rigid enforcement of nonfraternization edicts. The copter patrols were designed to spy on, intimidate, and frighten off American soldiers seen speaking with German civilians. But it was glorious summer after a fierce winter; and in the green fields outside shattered cities throughout Deutschland, young men and women were stretching hands toward one another. The copters were a dismal failure.

We were four characters in a prophetic scene from Absurdist Theater, which had not yet been invented. Wilhelmina and her sister, Clementina—Willie and Clem, naturally—two large, robust Fräuleins from Silesia, had allowed a friend and me to follow them from the wounded town to fields where they desperately searched for food. Refugees, they had fled before Russian troops into American lines, leaving behind parents and privilege. It was obvious they had known many advantages and comforts before Germany's defeat.

My amorous friend, Clare, was tolerated with amusement by the hearty sisters as they consumed berries and resolutely kept the conversation—in flawless English—on American literature and cinema. The war had deprived them of so many foreign books and films—had I read Hemingway's *For Whom the Bell Tolls*, did you see *Gone with the Wind* and was it as fine as they say? We joked a great deal, having learned to survive horror that way, but behind the merriment was stark terror. Talk of books forced Clem to speak of her parents' bombed home and library; Willie's good-humored rejection of Clare's flirtation prompted remarks, casual and fatalistic, of witness to rape and her own narrow escape. While our laughter drowned out the sound of the detested copter, the sisters' hands were busy picking strawberries and stuffing them into tattered kerchiefs. When Clare moved impulsively toward Willie to steal a kiss, she playfully smashed berries against his puckered lips, staining his face a bright blood red. And we stopped laughing. He was suddenly, unnervingly, too much like too many splintered faces we had seen during the brutal winter.

There's a motor in the sky now, a jet high above us, its plume trailed long and white against a turquoise sky. Daria has put her hand in mine, and I walk her to the house, savoring her happy, childish chatter of strawberries and birthdays and wonder in the world.

IT SEEMS to me now that the sun always shone on Easter morning. Memory is selective; but did the weather ever dare rain, sleet, turn gray or cold on such a special day? No. The dawn was glorious, sunrise brilliant; birds sang from the tops of leafing-out neighborhood trees; color blossomed in the nearby parks. One could smell the freshness and the new life.

I would stand by the window of a bedroom shared with one bachelor uncle and two motherless cousins (they slept on) and be essentially alone, within myself, welcoming the opening of this splendid day. The view was into adjacent yards, over a wide city alley and onto the backs of a long line of identical row houses. But it could have been Elysium. I was certain that He walked the earth, was very near and that—holding my breath!—He might come striding over those rooftops to touch me.

My mother's feelings were similar. She would be busy as ever in the kitchen—work hadn't dissipated, the Depression hadn't gone away—but her pre-breakfast songs had a special lilt to them. We shared the same joy that it was all over, the long weeks of a cold and harsh Lent, the fastings and denials, the surrender of amusements, the strict discipline of constantly conscious behavior permitting few concessions to human frailty. And especially this past week, with the power of the Passion so shattering: my hours at school frequently interrupted when the good nuns walked us, two by two, boys up front, girls behind, down the wide pavements and into the dark, hushed church—like all churches of its day, infinitely mysterious, comforting as well as a bit frightening, a place where miracles truly happened, all within yourself, astounding you with their mighty revelations and transformation—to the Holy Week services. Back to church at night for a Tenebrae featuring the extinguishing of candles one by one and flesh-crawling minutes in total darkness followed by a sudden, dramatic, searing illumination of the crucified Christ on His tremendous cross on the sanctuary wall. Mother silent, sometimes weeping, through the three hours on Friday. The radio stilled, piano untouched, conversation at a minimum through the evening. Death in the house, excruciatingly real, as real as those few times there had been a bier in the living room and I had approached it with gravity, fear, and fascination. Even our blasphemous menfolk, my fallen-away father and uncle, not only accepted the stark sorrow of the darkened home but silently, inwardly—uncomfortably—grieved.

There were sausages and eggs, Philadelphia scrapple, New York bagles, pastries, and—for kids who had touched no candy in six weeks —bowls of jellybeans and chocolates. All to be offered, promptly, to family members upon return from Mass and after the Communion fast had been honored. On the diningroom sideboard were Easter baskets for my sisters, nests artfully arranged from cardboard boxes, for my cousins and myself. Each was jammed with dyed eggs, sugared chicks and bunnies, ubiquitous jellybeans and cookies, all radiating from a singular grand mound of chocolate stuffed with coconut and jellied fruits and topped with our very own names in white icing. Once home from church, we were given a brief, dutiful homily on the anguish of bellyache, then licensed to demolish or hoard the goodies as we chose.

The girls spent considerable time admiring and parading in their new spring frocks. My cousins and I ventured outdoors into the challenging, sometimes devastating, local sport of "picking eggs." Already some of the neighborhood toughs were striding the streets with one hand holding aloft their champion hard-shelled egg, which had cracked the point or butt of other eggs—now resting in a bulging sack prominently displayed—for blocks around. These strutting boys, and an occasional revolutionary girl, sang their challenge from the middle of the street, where all would-be contestants, on porches or from behind lace-curtained windows, could see and hear them. "Who's got a guinea gee, who wantsa picka me." This was fairly blatant advertising, for professionals only. The guinea egg was generally thought to be much harder-shelled than the common chicken eggs used in most of our homes. But one never knew: sometimes a chicken egg could crack that bully's guinea, and the world had few sweeter pleasures than besting such wise guys. Of course, there was always the possibility that he had doctored the egg with resin, had been toughening its shell for a week or more. Anyway, Easter wasn't Easter unless you picked a few eggs—not just for fun, as you did with your sisters, but for keeps. If lucky, you might increase your nest by a few alien specimens, always different, the dyes somehow distinctive from ones originating in your own home. If unlucky, and you carried a losing streak to its bitter end, you were cleaned out. It was very easy to read in our faces, as the day wore on, which of us were victors and which the defeated.

A great-uncle arrived for the afternoon dinner. He had walked many miles (to save streetcar fare) from the old port where he continued to live in a dark walkup above a dilapidated store, disdaining the new uptown neighborhoods and their erosion of ethnic heritage in first-generation attempts to "become American." Unmarried, crotchety, smelling of the fermenting grapes he pressed in his room, notoriously penurious, Uncle Jake held great fascination for me. He was from "the old country," another world, different from everyone else I knew. On infrequent visits to his flat, I was deliciously intimidated by the colorful old neighborhood, the spooky climb up a dark, narrow stairwell to rooms cluttered with intriguing, mysterious piles and boxes of forbidden junk and treasures, lighted by flickering candles because electricity was expensive. I had heard Mother whisper about "that woman," apparently not virtuous, who came to see him; I always hoped to encounter her, but never did.

On Easter, Uncle Jake lined up the children and ceremoniously went through his annual ritual of having each of us hold out a small hand, into which he placed, with great solemnity, a shining new nickel. Our formal acceptance and response were well rehearsed, flawless, unmarred by giggling—which broke out only after his back was turned. I used to shadow him, not merely because he was foreign and exotic, but because in him I first suspected that love could be expressed through gruffness. Once, I secretly followed him on his lone, long walk to his apartment. When he discovered me, at a street-crossing blocks away from my house, his stern eyes quickly softened; and he took my hand and led me gently home.

Late on Easter evening, finally free of household chores, Mother would sit and welcome neighbors or relatives who had "just dropped in." Her interest in all of them was as impartial as her love for all of us. She was rarely alone, though some of us vied for her exclusive attention. One year I overheard a lady friend comment that she was to be pitied because of all the demands made on her time and energy. But a companion quickly countered, "Pitied? Maria? She lives a life of ministry! And like her Risen Lord's, it's surrounded her with disciples."

MAY

Intelligent, cultured, circumspect,
she had never until now flaunted
the conventions.

T HE WOMAN and I were both ignoring the dinner call and for-
feiting the first meal aboard the westbound *Vulcania* to remain on
the afterdeck as the ship plowed through the Bay of Naples. Busy
seamen urged us to go below, to get out of their way; meals were
scheduled at sailing time for the express purpose of keeping passengers
off the decks during the strenuous period of clearing the harbor. But
the woman and I stood motionless at the rail, our eyes riveted to the
receding shoreline.

We remained there together for such long minutes—past Cas-
tellammare, Ischia, and Capri, out of the Golfo and into the Tyrrhenian—that a strong, silent empathy developed across the space between us. I knew what was rending my own heart, the overwhelming
conviction of mistake in leaving a land fiercely loved for the purely
practical reasons of concluded studies and future employment. The
woman's anguish seemed no less intense than mine. When land could
no longer be seen, at the moment we had to surrender it, she turned to
me and suggested we go to the bar.

She was a missionary's wife returning to the States with him and
their two small sons after long years of service in the Philippines. Huk
terrorists had forced them to close their mission, and they were headed
to a new parish and assignment in the Middle West. "I don't think I
can face it," Lillian explained over the first drink. "Not middle-class

provincialism, pious patronage from ladies' church-circles toward the minister's wife, teas and committees, sanctimonious spinsters and fund raising. Not all that after the freedom of the islands!''

They had journeyed through Suez and into the Mediterranean, and she had looked forward to touring Italy during the week between ships. But her husband had installed her in a Naples hotel with the children and gone off alone to Rome. Passage on the *Vulcania* was to be her vengeance. "All my life I wanted to see the glories of Italy, and they ended up being the four walls of a shabby room. This voyage is mine! Jim, that most reverend, can spend it babysitting his sons in the stateroom.''

She carried no cash, and within a few hours my own meager reserve was gone over the bar. It was to have been a carefully budgeted fund for shipboard tipping and initial expenses on arrival at New York. But I was experiencing emotions not felt since wartime—we were casualties, walking wounded, battered buddies ministering to one another. And Lillian proved as strategic at requisition and appropriation as any combat comrade I had known. When my wallet yielded no more, she drew into our conversation a lonely, timid, exploitable young man, Junior, whose billfold was exceptionally well lined and who could always cable Daddy back in rural Indiana, ship-to-shore, when replenishment was necessary. Lillian, Junior, and I became an inseparable, unlikely trio for the entire time we remained at sea.

She was a cornered, frightened—not a designing—woman. Intelligent, cultured, circumspect, she had never until now flaunted the conventions. Her husband, Jim, whom we encountered on his infrequent visits topside, where he walked their two preschool boys, was an attractive, athletic, discerning man. He seemed predisposed to permit his wife this shipboard indulgence before meeting the heavy responsibilities of their new mission. But Lillian taxed even Jim's great patience, not joining him or their sons at meals, spending the long blustery days (it was a rough crossing) in the many bars and salons scattered throughout the ship, at the scheduled games, contests, sports, and crafts sessions, at the afternoon and evening movies, in the chic boutiques of First Class. Junior's wallet seemed bottomless. He gratefully opened it each time his senior companions, the urbane minister's wife or her world-weary war veteran, emptied another glass with him.

Lillian was prudent, never alone with Junior or myself, insisting on the threesome. At midnight, she would promptly excuse herself, like Cinderella at the ball, and return to her cabin. Toward the end of the trip, driven topside more frequently by increasingly bad weather, I saw more of Jim and grew to like him. Whatever their present differences, it was obvious that he and Lillian deeply loved one another and that he understood her temporary rebellion. He was no milktoast but a resolute, proud man, and I marveled at his controlled forbearance. But underneath the debonair exterior, I detected a seething volcano.

Junior suspected nothing. He reveled in the company of elders and the titillation from their acceptance of him. He grew bolder, and careless, and on our last night out persuaded Lillian to forget the midnight curfew. Agonizing over her imminent capitulation to the Babbitts of the Midwest, she lingered on. One and two o'clock passed while the three of us lounged in an otherwise deserted salon, I with some apprehension, smelling danger as surely as I had under the bombs of Antwerp or on the banks of the Rhine. When, after much fruitless argument that we disband, I rose to go off alone, Lillian, ever wise, refusing to remain in a compromising situation with one man, rose as well.

Climbing a grand stairwell, we linked arms in warm affection, three musketeers gravely acknowledging that our friendship and adventure were over. The morning would be taken up with hectic debarkation, and we would never see one another again. The rough sea and the night's libations caused us, eyes lowered, to watch our footing on the richly carpeted stairs. I think we all glanced up at the same moment. On a landing above us was Jim, incongruously outfitted with a walking stick and bright, striped pajamas. Standing at casual attention, he lifted the stick, drew from its hollow sheath a long Philippine bayonet, and raised the tempered steel ritualistic fashion, like a challenging knight-of-old, at arm's length before his face. Lillian lowered her hands from Junior's and my shoulders and went immediately to him.

I saw them last on the pier at New York sitting among a mountain of trunks, souvenirs, and trophies from the Pacific. They each held a child by the hand, and were beleaguered by customs officials. Both Lillian and Jim were shouting messages to me above the heads of the crowd, but I never heard them. The boys began a scrap, and their parents bent down to them, lost to view, letting me go from their lives while turning in unison toward domestic concerns.

HIGH AMONG my pleasures at dinner parties in our home are the table settings. It is always a pleasure to see the bold and successful arrangements that Ellen creates with seemingly incongruous china, crystal, and silver. Flaunting all rules, she combines fine porcelain with the humblest earthenware, contemporary with classical designs, chipped and fragile heirlooms with the sleekly elegant dinnerware of modern technology. It is a mysterious art to me. Like the unskilled layman in a picture gallery unable to analyze or dissect a favorite painting, I can only stand and marvel.

Not infrequently, guests will inquire about this or that unusual cup or platter. Nearly all have little monetary value but are dear to us through association. A friend brought this from Greece, and that was carried from Marrakech by someone who knew we'd like it. How many times did Ellen's mother pour coffee for me in the cup I now touch, and didn't her grandmother bring this saucer from New England? Often enough, the setting is a veritable genealogical table—

here's a spoon of vintage Americana beside a bowl that came in my grandmother's dowry from Sorrento. It is all part of a mystique I but dimly comprehend, no matter how great my aesthetic pleasure and appreciation of the art. Perhaps few men can really understand it.

Once, in a rustic German farmhouse, I stared with fascination at precise rows of shining china displayed against the rough boards of a hand-hewn hutch. The blue-patterned plates and cups held my attention because of their rigid formation and spotlessness. What were they doing, how had they survived a topsy-turvy world, where had any of us last seen such order? The room that housed them was extremely modest, next to a stable. At the moment, it was almost bare, most of its furniture stacked precariously atop a horse-drawn wagon just outside the door. Our advance unit had been ordered to appropriate the house as a battalion headquarters. We were evicting the owners, a grim old man and his weeping, white-haired wife.

The aged couple moved with exasperating slowness, befuddled by the confusion of language and the suddenness of this dispossession. In charge of the detail was a corporal who had been assigned the mean duty, even though there was higher rank among us. I watched his tortured face as he tried to explain to the Germans again and again why their household goods were being piled on the wagon; why they must leave immediately because it was already dusk and they could be shot on sight if seen on the roads after curfew; how an entire battalion would occupy the area by morning and this house would become a military headquarters. The old people sadly shook their heads, understanding nothing.

Someone remembered that the half-track driver spoke a little German and went to get him. The driver proved a lout who enjoyed teasing the elderly couple, tweaking them with his rifle as he explained the situation. He insisted that they understood his words even as they continued to tarry, the woman rocking her head in puzzlement. She was, he translated, mumbling about this crude house, how she'd lived here since her marriage, raised sons—now dead on two fronts—welcomed daughters-in-law and grandchildren. It was a long domestic litany of a family disbanded and possessions hard-won and lost. She and the old man were alone and didn't know where to go if we turned them out. "And it's that damned china," the driver mocked. "She keeps saying she can't have it on the wagon—it's fragile and will break. It's her wedding china."

I saw the conflict in the corporal's eyes. He had only recently attained that rank after many other promotions and subsequent busts, and failure in this mission would mean another demotion—would mean more humiliating, menial chores, such as he'd already had too much of. An agriculturist from a strict Calvinist background, his compassion for these rural Germans was obvious. The woman, I became aware, resembled pictures of his mother that he had shown me. And he tried at first, through the interpreter, to treat her as a son would, flattering, humoring, cajoling her to move toward the door. But each time her husband took her arm and coaxed her forward a few steps, she would stop and turn back to the cupboard. And finally she said No, she could not go, no one could make her leave her home and wedding china.

It was almost dark. I saw panic in the corporal, for violation of curfew could well mean the Germans' deaths by the hand of a nervous sentry. He tried one last time to ease the woman toward the door. She stood stubborn and firm, jaws set, eyes riveted on her cherished dishes. The corporal strode to the cupboard and with a quick sweep of his arm sent plates crashing to the floor, splintering against our ankles, settling on the worn planks in islands of gleaming fragments. "Tell her," he shouted at the driver, "that I'll smash them all unless she leaves; that if she hopes to find any of them left after we move out, she'll go this minute." The woman collapsed against her husband and permitted him to guide her outdoors. We helped them into the wagon, and set the scrawny horse at a tired pace down the darkened road. For a long time we could see their silhouettes against shellfire in the northwest sky.

The corporal lay with his face to the wall that night but did not sleep. When I put a canteen of schnapps in his hand, his fingers closed over it greedily, but he could not speak. In the weeks that followed, for so long as we stayed in those quarters, he let no one go near the cupboard; and each day he inventoried the remaining china.

A GENTLEMAN from Illinois is confused about New Mexico's patron of the fields, San Ysidro. A modern agriculturalist with an interest in iconography, he has visited Santa Fe's Museum of International Folk Art and the homes of woodcarvers in nearby Cordova. Like so many newcomers to the region, he is surprised and delighted by the excellent craftsmanship of traditional and contemporary New Mexican bultos. He has heard or read of most of the santos esteemed here—even Santo Niño de Atocha, little known outside areas of Hispanic heritage in the United States—but San Ysidro is news to him. "St. Isidore the archbishop of Seville, yes," he says, "but the woodcarvers tell me this is not the same man—no archbishop but a simple farmer. Is he strictly legend, or did such a person live?"

I take a reference volume, *The Saints*, edited by John Coulson, from a studio shelf and hand it to the man. There he finds listed five Isidores, among them the revered patron of Madrid, Spain, who has won wide devotion from all generations in New Mexico. Coulson is meticulous in distinguishing historic fact from fiction in his abbreviated biographies, and Ysidro's entry is limited to a few lines. "Born a Spanish peasant (*c.* 1130), he was yet able to give freely to the poor, living with his wife a life of such piety that both are venerated as saints."

More than as a man of charity, Ysidro is acknowledged as the man of prayer in the New World. The most popular legend tells us that his desire to pray was so great that the Lord sent angels to perform the heavy farm chores, freeing Ysidro for meditation and devotions. Numerous representations of him in paintings and carvings illustrate this traditional story. He is nearly always shown with two oxen, occasionally more, pulling a plow. Angels hover nearby, and in some of the paintings a church is visible across the fields. Ysidro most frequently holds the reins to the oxen, but I have seen charming santos in which the reins are slack, or nonexistent, and the saint's hands folded in prayer. Sometimes he looks totally lost to everything but spiritual thought, oblivious to the demands of crops stretching on all sides—after all, the angels can take care of them.

In addition to the San Ysidro land grant and the town of San Ysidro in Sandoval County, other small, unmapped communities in New Mexico honor the saint in place names. On a recent trip through the lower Rio Grande valley, I visited friends who live in an old and still obscure settlement dedicated to the saint. The area remains largely agricultural, and it is always a pleasure to look over irrigated fields flanking both sides of the Rio, stretching toward arid mountains east and west. My friends are proud of the acres surrounding their home, and particularly of their cotton crops. We rarely fail to step outdoors after a good dinner to watch the sun go down behind distant mesas, see its last fiery rays on the small adobe church across the furrows.

There is a modest but endearing bulto of Ysidro housed in that church, lovingly cared for by the local people and carried by them in procession through the fields on the saint's feast day each May. My friends, gringos who have lived in the valley for many years, attend church, join the annual procession, and are knowledgeable in regional lore. They told me where I erred in data about San Ysidro in one of my publications on santos.

He was not a man of the twelfth century, it seems, and apparently not from Madrid. For one of the valley's oldtimers, Pedro, tells a story handed down through generations of his family, which truly explains why Ysidro is patron of the fields. The humble saint was out planting corn one gray day, when he was startled to see a handsome, bearded man rushing breathlessly toward him. Obviously, the man was fleeing great danger. When he drew closer, Ysidro fell on his knees, recognizing Nuestro Señor, the Christ. Nuestro Señor stopped and rested a moment, explaining that the Romans were after him and wanted to crucify him. Before resuming his flight, he blessed Ysidro, commending him for his good and simple ways, and especially for his lifelong habit of truthfulness.

Nuestro Señor was hardly out of sight when Roman troops appeared. They surrounded Ysidro and demanded to know if he had seen the fugitive, that man called Messiah, pass by. In deep anguish, unable to lie, with eyes cast down in fear and sorrow, the poor farmer admitted he had. Then the Romans wanted to know when, how long ago. Ysidro, fingering the kernels of seed in his trembling hands, replied, "While I was planting the corn." He heard the soldiers grumble and, after a while, realized they were departing—back on the path they'd come from, and not in the direction Nuestro Señor had fled. Raising his eyes in relief and gratitude, Ysidro beheld a miraculous sight. His fields were green with towering stalks of corn, fully grown and ripened, their golden tassels shimmering under a dazzling sun.

I did not comment when my sophisticated friends finished their story, and they laughed at my discomfort—how can one deny such a beautiful legend in the face of cold historic fact? "There's no point in disbelieving it," my host insisted, "for Pedro himself told me this, and Pedro is a good man. And Pedro heard it from his father, who was also a very good man. And the truth, *mi amigo*, is not in books but on the lips of good men."

WE HAD EXPECTED the news for weeks, and now it was official. The war in Europe was over. Our field radios crackled with reports from world capitals, duty was suspended, an unusual inertia settled over Battalion Headquarters. Officers were not to be seen, and few enlisted men. Since they had nowhere to go and little to do—Eschwege offered few attractions—their absence was a mystery until, as the hours passed, they were observed alone in quarters in the tidy suburban homes we had requisitioned before hostilities ended.

The silence of Headquarters contrasted sharply with the wild celebrations we heard being broadcast from Times Square, Piccadilly, the Champs Elysées. Lights were going on again all over the world, but Americans in Germany remained trapped in darkness.

Sometime in late afternoon, I heard a sergeant express what must have been in all our hearts. "So now they send us to the Pacific. The only place it ends for us is the grave." He was a Pole, an ex-coalminer from Pennsylvania, hard drinker and carouser, and an excellent field soldier. He stood under the bright May sky, *unter der Linden* of a shockingly neat, peacefully rural bourgeois neighborhood, speaking to no one in particular, confronted by a disheveled, tearful Fräulein. The small group of us who had gathered around recognized the girl, a young refugee with whom he had taken up—how long ago, a lifetime ago?—somewhere west of the Rhine. She had managed to learn our location, survive the treacherous roads, walk or cadge rides in army vehicles, and was here to claim *Mein Mann.*

Stanley was bone tired. None of the girl's public, wailing declarations of love for him cracked that awesome fatigue. His eyes seemed not to see her, nor his ears to hear, and when a buddy suggested that he take pity on her—acknowledge her presence—he thrust the man aside and strode toward the house we had converted to a club. Inside, the bar had opened early in the day, and pitiful attempts to understand Victory, to celebrate it, were well under way.

The Fräulein, barred from following the sergeant onto property used by the American military, took a position on the front steps and buried her head in her arms.

A friend and I later wandered into the bar and joined our solemn comrades. Stanley was drunk, as were a few others at his table, but drinking throughout the room proceeded with ruthless silence among the men. A radio continued to blare the revelries in New York and London—soldiers and sailors dancing in the streets with their women, national holidays declared; the churches were full; the bands were playing and the crowds singing. A dogfaced top-sergeant suddenly sent his stein of beer smashing against the wall.

I left the bar, my friend following, and stood aimlessly in the back yard, where an elderly woman was setting out rows of vegetable seed. She looked at us—the enemy—with harsh resignation, igniting an angry defiance in the man beside me. Impulsively he strode toward the neighboring house, an abandoned home boarded up and posted Off Limits, reputedly once the residence of a locally prominent family. I watched with astonishment as the soldier used a piece of discarded pipe to rip protective boards from a low window. The German woman was calling for him to stop. He answered her with obscenities and was soon in the house. I followed him.

It had been basely looted, apparently by the Wehrmacht as well as by Allied troops. Nothing of negotiable value remained. I found myself in a library ankle-deep in the shredded books, letters and papers, shattered phonograph records, and smashed memorabilia of an absent owner who had obviously cherished literature, music, and family keepsakes. Torn pages from a photograph album nakedly brandished mute faces—and pieces of faces—from three generations; they stared into me with cold accusation. I fingered a broken meerschaum pipe and examined the fragments of lovely architectural drawings, studies of Greek temple columns. Postcards, a few intact and bearing cancelled stamps with the image of Hitler, were testimony to carefree holidays in the Tyrol and on the Rhine. A group picture of uniformed young men gave my stranger's eye no clue to the identity of a son on a distant front. Among the clutter on the floor, my probing toe nudged the ragged remains of diaries, yellowed newspaper clippings, a beribboned bundle of letters, a child's school tablet with its slashed, startlingly gay crayon-drawings.

My friend and I left empty-handed. And as he quietly, sternly replaced the window boards—under the watchful eye of the old woman bent over her gardening—I knew I had lost, perhaps forever, a concern for possessions, material treasures, which had always been part of me.

My friend was sick and threatening trouble—to commandeer a jeep and drive recklessly into the night—so I stayed by him, sitting on the top step outside the enlisted men's bar. Stanley's Fräulein lounged dejectedly below us, her frail body occasionally wracked by convulsive sobs. For as long as we sat there, the radio played; and we heard the songs and shouts of Victory continue till morning.

JUNE

"She's been bad and you're going to let her get away with it.
How'll she ever know the difference between right and wrong!"

A QUICK business trip takes me south to Las Cruces but allows no time to slip over the border into Old Mexico. I spend an enjoyable day working out problems on a commissioned shrine, seeing old friends, dining at a lovely home in Doña Ana. But the Mexico itch is persistent; though I am functioning in Las Cruces, my mind is on Juarez. And when I head back north to Santa Fe, I know a sense of loss at having foregone a short excursion.

Mexico has always been a magnet to this family. During our first winter in Santa Fe, Ellen and I devoured books on the Aztecs, Los Conquistadores, and the Mexican Revolution. That was the beginning of a continuing love-affair with Mexico. Perhaps because tourism was modest in the early Fifties (we were often the only *norteamericanos* around), or because we used their language, no matter how poorly, the Mexicans singled us out for flattering attention. We have been going back, whenever possible, ever since.

But gingerly. For years we avoided tackling the deep interior, restricting ourselves to the northern states of Chihuahua and Sonora. We came to know Juarez, Chihuahua City, Hermosillo, and Guaymas extremely well. As the family grew, each new baby was introduced to Mexico at a tender age, and the older children fell more and more under her spell. We ventured farther, to Durango and over the Devil's Backbone to Mazatlan, down the coast to Bahia Santiago and Manzanillo, over to Guadalajara. Adventures, and misadventures, piled up. Romantic ideas about the country inevitably gave way to more realistic ones—and we loved Mexico even more.

Finally, we felt ready for the capital. The excitement, beauty, and riches of that diverse and challenging metropolis seduced us immediately. We are probably captives of Mexico City for life. There, as well as at the beaches or in mountain villages, we find that children, babies, and dogs are great ambassadors, opening up varied and constant contact with town and country people. We have felt at home in Mexico for a very long time, and she has given us, as anticipated, a fuller understanding and appreciation of our own Southwest.

But, thank God, some of the mysteries endure. On our last trip, at a service station outside Allende, I was sharply reminded that all the world is not yet cast in the American mold.

We had stopped after a hard drive, were tired and thirsty, and I elbowed my way through a crowded café for the usual quota of Cokes. The doors of our Volksbus were thrown wide, and the kids spilled out, the poodle got walked, the stacks of gear and paraphernalia were displayed. I opened my Coke, found a fly floating on the surface, and poured the contents on the ground. And even as I did so, I became aware that an Indian couple, sitting less than twenty feet away, were closely observing every move we made.

It was late in the day and I was irritable, impatient for the children to finish their drinks so we could be on our way. We were the only Americans around—and conspicuous with our great bus and large family—but the crossroad was crowded with Indians from the surrounding countryside. Vendors were persistent in dangling trinkets under our eyes as I mechanically and gruffly waved them off. They circled the bus, peering in at our possessions, chuckling at the younger children and the dog, ingratiatingly displaying their most clever toys and souvenirs. I saw the smaller children's eyes grow large with desire, and was angry, for our funds were limited—though, it seemed, these

Indians assumed that every American was a millionaire. All the while, the couple sitting nearby continued to stare at us.

The man and the woman rose at the last minute, just before we were ready to drive off. They approached us in grave dignity, with no enticing smiles and no wares for sale held aloft. A sudden movement from the man startled me. He had put his fingers to his open lips in the universal gesture of wanting food. And for one, awesome split second we were eyeball to eyeball, each looking into the soul of an inscrutable stranger. He was younger than I had thought, though work and privation had etched deep lines into a face as classic and enigmatic as an Aztec carving. Something passed between our locked eyes, some primordial sense of brotherhood. But then the dog barked, and the Indian shied away; and I waved him aside while gunning the motor.

Driving on to Allende, I justified the hasty departure, deciding it all amounted to nothing anyway. The man probably didn't want money for food, after all, but for pulque. And one couldn't just keep giving handouts to everybody who came along.

But now I wonder.

A PUBLISHER who has come to our gallery for the purpose of reviewing advertising material cannot concentrate on the work before us. She keeps glancing from the layout in our hands to a few tourists who are casually viewing the exhibits. Tourists are no novelty to me, and I do not look up. But the publisher ignores all my efforts to conclude our editing task.

"Are this year's summer visitors more bizarre than usual?" she asks.

"I don't think so. You're just not accustomed to Canyon Road."

She grunts disagreement, and I resignedly follow her stare. It is focused on a woman of indeterminate age, blonde, exceptionally lean, barefooted, frozen in an angular stance before an abstract painting. The stringy hair is all the way down her otherwise naked back, and a few ragged bandanas have been knotted together to form some kind of halter across her boyish chest; faded, multi-patched jeans are worn low on the narrow hips and are decorated with bright roses jammed into a torn pocket—roses, I recognize, just picked from my own terrace. The woman is giving the abstraction more study than it probably deserves —it seems a simple thing to me—and occasionally mutters to herself or affects a grimace as some new facet of the work is revealed to her.

"Nothing unusual," I tell the publisher. "Let's finish our job."

"Look again."

The blonde is shifting her stance now, and I see there *is* something peculiar about her, some wagging signal, insistently beckoning at her slightest motion. I see the two old-fashioned wooden clothespins clamping the front of her jeans together, sassy antennae riding over the flat stomach. The publisher is gathering up her layouts, ready to leave, though our work is unfinished. She is thoroughly unhinged. "Never saw anything like it in my entire life!"

But I have—very much like it, except that my earlier subject of observation would have been called bohemian instead of hippie, and sported one clothespin, not two, in place of buttons. She had somehow wrangled a state job as hostess of a national youth hostel, the Castello San Giorgio at Lerici, on the Gulf of La Spezia, below Genoa. Students, teachers, and other impoverished breeds, scholars and artists from around the world, would enter the dark castello and slowly, fearfully, climb hundreds of steep, unrailinged stone stair-steps toward dormitories set up within the top parapets. Many of the tender travelers were expecting the same solicitude they had received from other hostel hostesses all over Europe. Instead, they emerged into blinding sunlight to be met by a feverish, outlandishly costumed, bleached blonde posed dramatically against her personal stage-prop, the blue Mediterranean. Hair streaming in the wind, cockles and shells clanking from any place they could hang, a fisherman's net flung over her shoulders and dragging behind like a royal train, with a chattering marmoset in the crook of one arm, she would advance to greet downy-faced sophomores from Peoria and Sioux Falls. "Welcome to the Bay of Poets, haunt of D. H. Lawrence, spot where Shelley drowned and Byron burned his body on the beach. I am your hostess, The Exotic Creature of the Sea."

She answered to no other name, and the boldest of us quickly learned that La Creatura Exotica del Mare had no intention of cooperating with anyone who didn't address her properly. She made no attempt to assign bunks, locate the faulty showers, or provide any kind of service. Most guests avoided her, but a friend with whom I was traveling—a good sculptor but an outrageously amateurish psychologist—played ardent fan to her histrionics and won us an invitation to a mid-day meal in her sacrosanct room. We brought the dinner—bread, cheese, fruit, and wine—and had to share it with the marmoset when he was not admiring himself in his personal mirror or shrieking at the doves that flew in and out the open windows and arches.

The large, handsome room, stark-white walls with red-tiled floors, was empty of all furniture. Full drapes billowed wildly at the doorways, and a few pillows were scattered in the center of the floor. Three photos, one each of Lenin, Picasso, and our hostess (much younger, standing—inevitably—in the surf), broke the vast expanses of bare wall. La Creatura del Mare ate little, preferring to let the marmoset take food from her lips; she danced for us, badly, in a frantic contest with the doves, which she provoked into hysterical flight; and she talked incessantly, trying to win us (without success) to some secret brotherhood of the soul that would set everyone free. Alternating between French and Italian, she startled us with the repetitive use of one rare English word she had learned—*solipsist*. "I am a solipsist. We must all become solipsists."

My friend, always debative (and fond of wine), argued the case for human community. He grew abusive, suggesting that La Creatura's way of life was not an exploration of self, but an insane fantasy, some mad retreat from reality. He rampaged, demanding to know what she was hiding from, what horrors of the past, and present, had driven her to this crazy castle over the sea and a meaningless existence in illusion. For only a few seconds, she trembled violently under his attack; then she swooped up the marmoset and fled the room. Through the rest of that day and till after nightfall, all of us on the parapets of Castello San Giorgio could look down and see her standing in the sea, letting the waters heal her.

I have old, brittle movie-film of La Creatura, but even this evidence does not make her believable to most people. Her strangeness in those silent frames is perhaps totally unacceptable, much more easily (and comfortably) explained away as vagaries of faulty film, an unsophisticated camera, and the technical pitfalls of photographic exposures in Mediterranean light. The movie and these words—no matter how extravagant they seem—are merely tamed reflections of what she really was, way out there, beyond the pale.

THE COCKTAIL PARTY is in high gear. Host and hostess flow with practiced ease among the crowd of standing guests, glasses are quickly replenished, and the buffet features superb New Mexican delicacies. Ladies are resplendent in diverse fashions spiked with the occasional, brilliant flash of Mexican skirt or shawl. The men drip silver and turquoise jewelry as profusely as the women. Fragrant piñon logs burn in adobe fireplaces in every room, and through glass walls one can see the last of a spectacular sunset staining Santa Fe a fiery red. The evening chill is sharp, but I step outdoors for a brief respite from motion and talk, and to savor the color on the mountains, that awesome crimson which gave us the name Sangre de Cristo.

For only a moment, I know again the power and beauty of that mystery—that enigma, this land—which brought me to and holds me in New Mexico. The reverie is shattered by rough voices at the far end of the portal, two men loudly arguing Watergate. Their angry words are obscenely indifferent to a landscape flooded with mystical light and a Presence as real as the rocks and trees. I try to close my ears until the brief phenomenon ceases, the light is gone, and night descends.

But the vile conversation continues as one of the men, a politician I recognize, insists that we must now "forget Watergate, let the President get the country moving again." Everyone knows such things exist, the trick is in not getting caught; we must be pragmatic, seal the wound, and begin to recuperate. There can be no resignation or impeachment.

There is no mention of responsibility or guilt. I surrender my moment in the dusk, enter the house, and accept the drink immediately thrust at me.

Another night, another home; four of us sit ignoring a flickering television screen as one more casual discussion builds toward debate. Two of my friends are priests from out of state, the third a salesman of religious arts from the New York area. The priests had expressed the desire not to "talk shop, we're on vacation," but within minutes we are evaluating Vatican II, renewal, Church policy on birth control, abortion, and celibacy. Priests and laymen share much in common about these reputedly controversial and explosive topics. It is only when we come to the concept of sin, a word and subject carefully avoided among progressives in and outside the Church of the Seventies, that anger and vituperation soil our rhetoric.

The priests are disappointed that the salesman and I recognize serious wrong in ourselves and others; that we find evil a society that continues not only to tolerate but to foster wars, materialism, political skulduggery, prejudice, licentiousness, and brutality. Evil, it seems, is a four-letter word much less acceptable than those vulgarities we now hear in the best circles. And rare, the priests tell us—few people are guilty of serious wrong, they're merely weak, commit regrettable actions divorced from evil intent. (Are we all, then, Watergates?) Haven't we yet discarded the God of Wrath; haven't we heard the good news of Christian love and brotherhood, gentleness, joy, the kiss of peace?

We've heard it all. And endorse it all. But not without that other side of the coin, the harsher imprint of responsibility, discipline, sacrifice, and pain. We recognize no easy dogma that casually excuses our transgressions while we rock on with arias from *J. C. Superstar* and *Godspell.* We demand accountability in place of permissiveness. The salesman has mentioned an acknowledged rapist whom the courts turned loose on a legal technicality.

The television has been switched off and we grow quiet, grave with the problems of compassion and forgiveness, punishment and retribution. We are none of us adamant men, and slowly find our way back to less impassioned debate. In civilized, modulated tones, we begin to discuss the relative merits on both sides. But the gulf remains—spiritual leaders (like the politicians) who talk a soft leniency; laymen demanding tougher recognition of personal liability from church and state.

Days later, I am working in my studio when I hear a quarrel break out between our two young daughters. We're the only three in the house, and I'm reluctant to leave my work and go referee. Maybe they'll just stop if I ignore them, maybe the trouble will simply go away. But they do not quiet down, the din grows worse, and soon the older child is at my side, reporting what her younger sister has done.

I mutter noncommittal bromides as my hands remain busy with a small sculpture. But then a few of the child's words reach my mind, so stubbornly intent on design of line and form. "She's been bad and you're going to let her get away with it. How'll she ever know the difference between right and wrong!" I put down the modeling tools and follow my daughter toward the girls' bedroom.

MY UNCLE MACK held a pilot's license for traffic on the Chesapeake Bay, infrequently taking me with him for a day's outing on his launch. It was a small but sturdy craft, with compact cabin behind a husky prow, an open afterdeck housing the erratic engine and low benches port and starboard. It was no sporting vessel but a tough little working boat hauling provisions—usually butchered meats, fish, other foodstuffs—from markets in the port of Baltimore to ships anchored out of the harbor, often far down the Bay. For my purposes, the farther the better.

Uncle Mack took me along for companionship, but we had to work at it. He was a bachelor; we shared a room in my parents' home, and we did not always see eye to eye. A feisty bantam, pragmatic, popular with the ladies, *muy machismo,* his determined, strong, and uncompromising behavior brought him many friends and lots of enemies. No shrinking violet, Mack was controversial, never unnoticed, feverishly loved or hated. Striving to be a dutiful nephew, I had to strike a balance between those extremes while maintaining my own integrity. Wary of everything fanciful, esoteric, or mystical, my uncle preferred to put his trust in the concrete, what he could see and touch. He couldn't understand how a chunky kid who'd made the football, wrestling, and swimming teams at school, who reveled in soccer, could waste his evenings over drawing, reading, or listening to classical music. He'd knock that out of me if I'd let him. But we were evenly matched, and our frequent clashes nearly always ended in a draw.

It was on the launch that we most enjoyed each other. He was an excellent navigator, never careless, and the crowded harbor kept him busy. Little time to quarrel. I would crawl out to the end of the bow, straddle the forepeak, let the wind and spray batter my face. When we passed familiar landmarks—Fort McHenry, Sparrows Point, Gibson Island—they became, glittering in the sun or half hidden in the fog, ports in the Pacific, Indian and African seas, far-away places and strange-sounding names, calling, calling me.

We would shout back and forth about the landmarks or passing ships, and I would catch my uncle watching me with a curious eye. This, I think, he understood—this daydreaming, this fantasizing, as opposed to that I found in books and art. This was valid; a boy could —should—dream of adventure.

We would lunch aft while the engine idled or, very rarely, squander time by docking at an island. I preferred to eat on the launch, my uncle all the while inspecting the boat, swearing loudly at anything he uncovered that needed attention or maintenance. He was a different man on the water, liberated from the vanities and pretensions he displayed ashore with an endless stream of stricken ladies, free from the competitiveness that made him challenge other men. And free too of a soft sentimentality that lurked just under the surface of the thick hide, occasionally bursting forth to demolish him. Here on the water, all artifice was gone; and I was privileged to see the naked man, a salty and intelligent sailor marvelously transfigured by elements in which he recognized something beyond the tangible.

Surely I, too, will go to sea, I used to think, sensing no conflict between a mariner's life and the arts. For my maternal heritage was crowded with seamen, and a beloved grandfather had served a hitch in the Italian navy as a deep-sea diver. I had known him only as a gentle, sensitive, wine-sipping lover of opera, Chaplin, literature, and quiet pursuits. He had been many things—scholar, seminarian, immigrant —but it was always difficult for me to imagine him in the cumbersome diving-suit and helmet of the late nineteenth century. Intrigued, I constantly conjured up that image long after his death.

My uncle rarely spoke of his father, for Mack's pugnacious ways had caused problems between them. But sometimes on the Chesapeake, late in the day, when I was fighting sleep, he would speak more to himself than to me of the old man and his love for Sorrento and the Bay of Naples, and of all the uncles and cousins still there, going to sea, sailing the oceans, seeing the world. Mack swore he would go back to his father's land someday, would visit that place he'd heard so much about, try to understand its pull on him. But he never did. And when we had touched shore, he would surrender these indulgences, square his shoulders, and meet head-on the harsh realities of the moment.

One foggy day, sometime after my grandfather's death, when Mack had been out alone on the Bay, he came home unusually early, ashen and shaken. He sat in my mother's kitchen, barely able to speak, confused, grieving, floundering. She had never seen him like that—a brother who was normally all cocky assurance, bravado, intolerant of weakness and fancies, dukes perpetually raised against every threat that might come down the pike of God's lusty, brawling universe.

"He was walking on the water, Maria," Mack murmured after a while. "Pop—coming out of the fog straight toward my boat, wagging a finger, reprimanding me. Walking on the water, and as real and as close to me as you are now."

My mother used to say that Uncle Mack was never quite the same after that. The man who had known all the answers began to ask questions. Eventually he gave up the launch and no longer put to sea.

JULY

Oh, hell, once—just once—relinquish the work ethic,
abandon weekend chores, and let the day seduce you.

WITHIN the space of one hour, two groups of tourists in the studio have requested schedules for the Santa Fe Opera and sought my advice concerning purchase of tickets, directions to the amphitheater, and suggestions about dress. The first couple, young, are neophytes to the art, approaching it with great trepidation, apprehensive that the experience will somehow be "too much for them." Recognizing in them a familiar mistrust and fear of the arts that I have often seen and never understood, and wanting to lead them gently toward something that could permanently enrich their lives, I suggest they attend performances of *Bohème* and *La Grande-Duchesse.*

The second couple, middle-aged, are summering here and eagerly looking forward to the American premiere of *L'Egisto.* Longtime buffs, they want opera new and old, and their frequent travels are usually determined by news of the music world. From Sante Fe in late September, they go on to Rome and concerts for which they already hold reservations. "We plan a few Holy Year activities as well," the man explains. "Have you heard the choir of Santa Cecilia?"

Except on commercial recordings, no. And has a quarter-century already passed since the last Holy Year—that Rome of 1950, Rome of so few automobiles, when the great piazzas could still be viewed as marvels of design and perspective, not cluttered parking lots; where one heard the murmur of singing fountains, not Klaxons and exhausts; where then as now, saint and sinner were drawn irresistibly into the enfolding arms of the Bernini colonnade, into the vortex of that splendid public piazza dedicated to San Pietro.

Rome and opera, St. Peter's Square and a prima donna. A friend and I had decided one eleventh hour, after finding no accommodations at any of the city's inexpensive hostelries and *pensiones,* to lounge on the hard stones under the Colonnade. Impoverished pilgrims from all over the peninsula and Sicilia were doing the same. Unlike them, we were not in Rome for spiritual purposes but to acquire student travel-visas permitting us to journey into Russian-occupied territories of central Europe. But even though I had not come to the Tiber on a religious pilgrimage, I found myself continually drawn toward the Vatican. Paul tagged along reluctantly. And with much grumbling, we settled down for a night's rest at the base of a column, because, he mocked, "there's no room for us at the inn."

We were immediately approached by a lean, handsome Roman of poetic mien who proved anything but romantic. Roberto was, in fact, in the procurement business and could guarantee rooms if one accepted the amenities that came with them. Innocents abroad, we declined. Roberto was not easily put off, thoughtfully considering other ways to earn a commission from us. Exploiting our fatigue and sleepy vulnerability, he persisted with suggestions until we wearily followed him to a nearby neighborhood and the apartment of *una signora respettabile,* La Rosa. There, he promised us, were sofas of softest down that could be made up with immaculate linen, acceptable to the most fastidious American standards. The sofas were indeed soft and the linens immaculate, but we got little rest. La Rosa was too fascinating to forfeit to sleep.

She was old—the heavy rouge, hennaed hair, and flirtatiousness could not belie it. And age saturated her rooms, as well as her person, blatant in the walls covered with thickly patterned crimson damask, the glass-domed *objets d'art,* the silken dressing screens, towering potted palms, fringed cushions, exotic carpetings, and beaded doorways. Most of all in the huge paintings, richly framed in gilt and individually lighted, which graced every wall. They were all of a beautiful, youthful La Rosa in varying costumes—Tosca, Carmen, Violetta. *"C'est moi,"* she announced, standing proudly in her tattered flaming robe before each of the portraits. "I am an artist. In the theater!"

Once Roberto had departed after a whispered transaction over an exchange of lire, La Rosa brought linens and was about to retire. But Paul or I said something that betrayed us as sculptor and painter, and she quickly suggested a midnight *apéritif.* Fruit, bread, and wine appeared. We squatted on the floor around a glass-topped coffeetable illuminated by a spiraling brass candelabrum, while La Rosa retreated into past decades, humming an aria, reciting lines. Candlelight was kind to her, blurring the wrinkles cracking through caked cosmetics, the sagging flesh, time's ravages. She became less pathetic. We could almost glimpse the girl in the paintings, sense the steel behind those luminous eyes blazing from each canvas. She told us that she had starred in the opera for only a few seasons, then switched to "legitimate theater" and nonsinging roles. She hadn't worked for many years but was now and forever, first, last, and always, an Attrice. "A pariah to everyone else but fellow artists, comrades like yourselves." By dawn, we comrades had to abandon her—bowing gracefully stage center in an arched doorway—and stagger to the sofas in collapse.

I heard her singing as she prepared a noon *espresso* for us. No grand aria but a sentimental tune, *Italia mia,* popular then. Her voice was firm, strong, and very melodic. It brought a haunting dignity into that vulgar room. When I asked her, before we left, why she had deserted opera, she replied with a shrug and a few carefully enunciated words: *"L'amore.* What else? I had the talent but not the discipline, straying off wherever my heart led me." She embraced us, sighing *Addio, adieu,* and *auf Wiedersehen,* her physical release of us a lingering, tremulous farewell to arms, hands, fingertips.

I ran into Roberto once more before we left Rome, plying his trade as usual within the shadow of St. Peter's. When I thanked him for introducing us to La Rosa, admitting she'd touched me in a strange, unforgettable way, he brutally dismissed her as a washed-up has-been. Why didn't I get wise to the fact that Rome was full of much more interesting people and he could introduce me to all of them?

THE GENTLEMAN from El Paso is disappointed not to find a St. Christopher among the bronze medallions featured in our gallery. "You're like everybody else," his sudden attack begins, "canceling out San Cristobal simply because the Vatican arbitrarily decides to demote him. I expect more integrity from artists!"

The man's seniority in age does not deter my quick anger or defense. I argue that I have no Christopher medallion merely because I've never gotten around to designing one; that I've continued Christopher designs in tile despite all pronouncements from Rome; and furthermore that, to my understanding, Christopher has not been "demoted" but only removed from the Roman Universal Calendar, a change suggesting that his feast date need not be celebrated in countries where he's not generally known or esteemed.

"And just where in the whole wide world might that be?" the stranger demands. Black eyes flashing anger, short stature drawn up to imperious height, the proud heritage of Mexico vibrant in his crescendo-ing voice, he wags a finger at me and instructs me on Cristobal. "Even his origin is universal, no record of where he was born, with many countries claiming to be his birthplace."

"The problem with Christopher is precisely that," I reply. "Too many legends, too little historic fact."

"Legends are rooted in fact, in the essence of things. Did you know that Offero—as Cristobal was called before his conversion—was a

gentle giant in search of truth, like so many of our travelers today?
And that he had vowed to seek out, find, and serve the greatest king in
the world? He served more than one earthly king before discovering
that they were all subservient to someone else—Satan—and so Offero
served him. But then he learned that Satan stood in awe of a greater
king, El Cristo, and Offero began his long and hard journey to find
Nuestro Señor."

I had read that story and many others, including the most popular
one, of the saint's ferrying a small child on his shoulder across a
treacherous river. When the child proved to be Christ, Offero became
Christ-Offero—Christopher—the bearer of Christ.

"Yes, yes," the gentleman accedes, "at least it's obvious you do
your homework. Why, then, can't you make San Cristobal medallions? All travelers need them. Don't you?"

We had one, once, pinned on the windshield-visor of our car as we
drove through Mexico. Reluctant to leave that country we love so well,
we detoured on the way home, deserting the main highway at Los
Mochis for a run to Topolabampo and a seafood luncheon at the
Yacht Club. Entering Topolabampo, we saw that a road to the Yacht
Club was under construction but that the present and only route to it
was a narrow dirt path climbing and twisting along the edge of a cliff
over the sea. To our horror, cars that had not made the grade (their
license plates from every southwestern state) were stacked, in pathetic
disrepair, at the foot of the first long ascent. But locals assured us that
Si, señor, the road was navigable, taxis from town did it every day.
Vaya con Dios.

I was in the passenger seat and Ellen was driving, or we just might
have abandoned the Yacht Club with its acclaimed seafood. But few
hazards intimidate my wife from what she wants, and up we went. She
maneuvered the car well, shielded on her inward side of the road from
what I was witnessing on the outward side—gravel and earth slipping

from beneath our right front tire over the side of the cliff into the Sea of Cortez. The children roared in real, not feigned, fright and delight.

The Yacht Club was beautiful, the food superb, the view of the sea incomparable. A few taxis from Topolabampo arrived, disgorging white-faced gringos who staggered into the diningroom and clutched at margaritas. My own consumption of margaritas was limited by the knowledge that I would have to drive the road back. Perhaps anxiety was responsible, when we were again under way, for my leaving that narrow path and entering a short but steep, dead-ended runaway exit carved in the side of the hill. This detour necessitated a hair-raising backup of the car high above the sea. By now the children were shrieking wildly, thoroughly enjoying adventure and danger. Halfway down our final descent, we met one of the courageous taxis on its way up. There was nothing to do but look for the nearest bulge in the slender lane, edge into it hugging the cliff face, hope the Mexican driver had been in this situation before and knew what he was up to, and trust we would all be spared disaster. There was rampant hysteria in our car, the children's loud, tremulous laughter battering against my ravaged nerves. As the taxi passed us, I saw, eyeball to eyeball, its passengers' terrified expressions, all tensed for the first thundering crunch of metal and an unscheduled dip in the sea. My foot ached from braking. At that moment, the St. Christopher medallion tore loose from its mooring on the windshield visor and crashed noisily to the floor. In unison, the children cried: "He's given up—even *he's* given up!"

"But obviously he hadn't," the gentleman from El Paso comments, "or you'd not be here to tell this inspiring story. I'll make certain my children and grandchildren hear it when I return home."

We part with warm handshakes and a genuine desire to see each other again. But he cannot resist a final word of counsel: "Don't let Rome tell you what saints are or are not universal. Make San Cristobal medallions."

WE LIVE in the mountains and often go down to the desert, but our family is inordinately fond of the sea. The oldest son is studying marine biology at college; the younger boy is a strong swimmer and, when seven years old, aided in his own rescue from treacherous currents off the coast of Mexico. Our grown daughter recently returned from San Francisco, where she was looking over schools and enjoying the Bay. Her smaller sister will body-surf in the roughest waves, and our youngest was carried aboard the *Cristoforo Columbo* at age three weeks to begin her first Atlantic crossing.

Ours is a home where boating magazines lie next to my references on cacti, and where scaled ship models crowd New Mexican geodes on bedroom shelves. Any television broadcast of Jacques Costeau's oceanographic adventures tops all other family activity, as parents and children converge from far corners of the house for a rare gathering before the tube.

We're good sailors, Ellen the best among us, but the Tyrrhenian Sea gave us quite a trouncing during an overnight trip from Sicily to Naples. We had boarded a listing passenger ferry at Messina in fairly good weather, then hit rough seas as soon as the harbor was cleared.

The *Lipari* was not much of a boat, especially below, where we were forced to spend most of the night in a dark, airless cabin. The open decks were quickly deserted of vacationing school teachers, students, hippies, and other budget-minded travelers who had staked out benches and chairs in anticipation of an evening under the stars. Surly (and frightened) seamen kept everyone below with sharp, colorful expletives straight out of *The Godfather*.

Loving the sea and despising our wretched cabin, Ellen and the boys argued to stay topside. But the small boat rode those monstrous seas like a beserk car on a roller coaster. Passengers were thrown into bulkheads, or pitched down stairways; seamen worked the decks on safety lines. Teenagers who had refused to stay below were swept off their feet and battered against the railings; and they had to be retrieved. I was warned that our Volkswagen bus, lashed to the open bow, would probably be swept overboard. And I could not have cared less, fully occupied in seeing that a rebellious family remained in that foul cabin.

When we came into harbors, lying at anchor off Vulcano, Stromboli, or Panarea, there was respite. The full complement of passengers, white-faced and nauseated, came into the open air, hoping the boat would never leave these relatively calm waters. But once it discharged departing islanders in long-boats and took on more for the mainland, the silly little vessel plunged again into the maelstrom.

Traveling with us was a business partner, a good friend from Milano, Angelo Marelli. A gentle man, he had accommodations worse even than ours—a multi-tiered dormitory that housed quarreling, sick strangers. We would meet him on deck at "ports-of-call," all of us breathing deeply of fresh air. If seasickness can be measured, Angelo was the sickest in our group, but he never failed to check out the children, counting heads, or reach inside the baby blankets I tightly clutched, making certain Daria, not yet four months, was still with us.

Seasoned travelers who rarely vacation but go on trips for work or study, my family can turn the most discomforting (and harrowing) experiences into adventure. Though all hated the stifling cabin below deck, we took keen interest in the sightings and calls. The children were fascinated by the heavy long-boats, poled by powerful men with broad, bare feet firmly balanced on rocking gunwales. These stout boats carried islanders, young as our Daria and old as Methuselah, across choppy waters, while relatives on distant wharves linked arms and chanted farewells.

The songs, primal, more Greek than Italian, more pagan than Christian, were like caresses, tender laments of parting wafted over wide waters. We watched the tough Aeolians, including women and the aged, leap with agile grace from long-boat to the *Lipari*, hand over dogs, birds, and sundry other pets, baskets and hampers, battered suitcases and string-tied boxes, all with gruff efficiency and speed.

At Panarea, undiscovered by the jet-set but a jealously guarded summer haven for industrialists and the wealthy of Milan and Turin, we took on the "beautiful people" with their scuba gear, small sailing craft, guitars, transistor radios, high fashion, and one Ferrari to keep company with our Volks, miraculously still lashed topside in the bow.

At every island call, we lingered as long as possible on the decks, not only for the air and to avoid our cabin, but to marvel at those awesome volcanic peaks thrusting up from the sea, to remember Ulysses' surrender to ancient lures, watch the fireballs on the dark slopes of Stromboli and hear their hissing cascades to the sea.

At one such moment, I stood at the rail with Angelo Marelli, who was ashen, trembling, pitifully seasick. Regretting that we had influenced him to come on this voyage (his original plan was a train from Reggio), I cursed myself, the *Lipari*, all boats, and inclement weather. But Angelo raised a hand to still my words. "Ah, no," he said, "the train would have been comfortable, and I would be safe and not ill. But that would only have been a routine trip. This is poetry!"

We limped into Naples next morning under sunny skies. The cars were still on the bow; none of us had suffered a bruise. Our crew was gathered around an early morning newspaper that had been handed up from the dock, and I saw the headline—another boat of similar class had gone down in the storm. Ruan, who was 10 and now knew everything there was to know about going down to the sea in ships, was scandalized at the newspaper story. A cowardly captain, sacrificing lives, had abandoned his sinking vessel. Ruan then and there instructed us all on international naval regulations and ethics.

IT IS HIGH SEASON and the Jersey beach is crowded, acres of distressingly pale or envied browned flesh lolling under gaudy umbrellas, frolicking and resting on the sands, splashing in the sea. Here is sun, and leisure, the change of pace, the late summer respite before the inevitable chills of autumn. Here the working man and woman—with family—wallow in the seductions of the annual vacation, two weeks at the seaside, freedom from the treadmill, routine, and responsibility. Here all summer in a bright, burning world without timeclocks, deadlines, or restraints. From one end of the beach to the other, the air sings with happy shouts of laughter; and all the wet or oiled faces are wreathed in unfettered smiles.

But liberty is compromised at the water's edge. The surf has been running rough, there are riptides; lifeguards herd all bathers and swimmers into restricted areas of the immense sea. A woman had drowned here only a few days earlier, and the guards are anxious, their constant warning whistles calling back bathers who wander beyond the farthest breaker or drift outside invisible boundaries established by the beach patrol.

For three successive days I take two young children into the pounding surf. Resentful of barriers, particularly in the expanse of oceans, I nevertheless conform to regulations. These are unfamiliar shores, and credence must be given those natives who habitually frequent them. The children and I, so accustomed to less democratic diversions, sport among the populated breakers, occasionally crashing against the slippery bodies of strangers. Like them, we jockey for positions that will carry us unimpeded on the crest of the next wave.

The sea rolls in relentlessly. I do not stand in the surf but let my knees touch the shallows, remaining at the children's level, rising and falling with them as the waves propel us toward shore or carry us away from it. The youngsters are fearless, secure under the eyes and touch of their father. Faces pressed one against the other, we watch each approaching wave build higher and higher, a high wall of rushing energy arching splendidly above our heads before crashing down to catapult us forward. For a few moments, we lose the sun, tumbling with tightly closed eyes in foaming brine, my arms around the younger child, the older one clutching my swimsuit with a small fist. We surface laughing, exhilarated together in play.

There are calmer minutes during which the sea seems to catch her breath, pushing shoreward gentler swells that cradle us like tender babes. We float or paddle with the rocking rhythms, buoyed with very little effort, at one with the flow of the tide. I enjoy the surcease from challenge and combat, content to let the quieter elements anoint me, but the children are quickly bored, looking hopefully out to the horizon, awaiting a livelier change of pace.

We can see the huge wave coming a long way off. It is building in momentum and height and will certainly break directly upon us. The children steel themselves for it with delicious apprehension, squealing with a terror that is all mockery, supremely oblivious to any genuine threat. A parent is in the sea with them, and strong, browned lifeguards remain alerted on the beach. The on-rushing wall of water is the biggest, best wave yet, will hit us harder than all the rest, provide the grandest thrill!

It shuts out everything else—other bathers, sea and sky, the rest of the world. Facing it from a child's level, I see nothing but the white-capped wave racing to engulf us. Then it is poised high above our heads; and for the split second before it descends, I am robbed of vacation laxity and mentality. The wave is a symbol of the greatest fears and threats we shall ever know, the sudden, monstrous, crushing onslaughts that batter us after deceptive calms, turning our worlds topsy-turvy.

We are under water, billowing swiftly God-knows-where in a black space of speed, force, and thundering noise. My arms tightly hold one child, but the other's been torn away—I feel her hand wrenched from my swimsuit. Then we strike sand, cast up at the very edge of the sea, lying in frenzied eddies of white foam. The children, surprisingly sobered—has the sport become a bit too rough even for them?—cling to me. The smaller child seems on the verge of tears. But when I ask why, it is not because of fear of the sea, merely that the huge wave has stripped her of bathing pants. We quickly retrieve them.

Lying warm and drowsy on a blanket spread over golden sands, we resist surrendering the nearly deserted beach after most bathers have responded to the dinner hour. The lifeguards have gone for the evening; the folding-chairs and umbrellas are absent; only a few people (inlanders like ourselves?) sit staring over the ocean or amble along the shore. One lone intrepid swimmer walks into the surf well out of the safety zone no longer demarcated on the unpatrolled beach. He stands for a long moment surveying the vast stretches of turbulent water. The sea appears dark, mysterious, cold, and treacherous. Emptied of the playful humanity romping in it only an hour earlier, devoid of dazzling sunlight that had shimmered on colorful bathers, murky under a pale sunset, the Atlantic commands respect with its awesome invincibility. The swimmer raises his arms above him, silhouetted in ritualistic salute to the dominance of the sea, before plunging into a baptism against the formidable and the unknown.

SUNDAY AFTERNOON, and it is very still—high sun, few clouds, little wind, the streets deserted by residents and tourists who have fled to the cool mountains. Our house is unusually quiet, with the older children off to fun and games, mother at the chamber-music concert, the smallest child collapsed in a rare nap. The dog dreams whimperingly under a patio table, and the cat luxuriates in a blazing patch of sun. Oh, hell, once—just once—relinquish the work ethic, abandon weekend chores, and let the day seduce you. The redwood chaise under the pear tree is irresistible.

I have scarcely closed my eyes when I feel small fingers on my brow. Daria has wakened and, not valuing silence or solitude as her father does, is seeking company. She is troubled by the absence of mother and siblings, the strange aspect of her home without sound and action. Instinctively sensitive to my mood, she makes no demands but strokes my temples and traces gentle patterns down the bridge of my nose.

Soon I feel her on the chaise, nestling into the crook of my arm. Her chatter begins, slowly at first because Daddy's tired and she's shrewd enough not to push things too fast when there's no one else around to play with. Do I know that ladybugs are good for flowers because they eat aphids, and you shouldn't hurt them? One is on her brother's personal rosebush but there's none on hers and she's thinking of transferring it. She saw an enormous worm this morning, and it makes tunnels under the ground, giving the earth air. Did I see how many squash are under the bushes or how big the grapes are getting or that more strawberries are ripening? What made those tiny seeds we planted grow so tall—"bigger than me!"—and when do I think we can eat their corn?

At four, it is her summer of discovery. The garden is a magical world of insects and plants, strongly competitive to toybox and swings. I am pleased to make her a gift when a few isolated clouds pass overhead. For she has never before been instructed in cloud-watching, and she marvels at the pictures I point out to her. She squints at the brilliant sky, trying to interpret shapes as Daddy does. Her celestial Rorschach is extremely simple—everything is white poodle or shrouded ghost.

She's on my stomach now, energy building, voice rising, her sturdy frame grinding against rib and femur. I see the blond hair edged with sunny gold and ringed by turquoise heavens, the delicate profile soft as that of a Raphael angel but animated with mischievousness, wit, and precociousness. She's jumping on me now, absolutely secure in her rights and my tolerance.

The cat has stirred and decided to check the lily pond—one never knows when some foolish goldfish might surface. Daria jumps from the chaise and goes to the rescue, shooing cat and lifting the edges of water pads to see if the minnows are still around. Ruan and Chiara netted them on a jaunt to Lake Fenton, where Daria's summer of discovery took giant steps. She had never been out in a boat on a lake and vastly enjoyed my labored rowing. The small, inflatable rubber raft is one her brother purchased in Ventimiglia four years ago and brings home from college on summer vacations. It has been paddled off the Italian mainland, Sicily and Mexico, but usually not by me. Essentially a one-man vehicle, it seemed to me crowded even with one tiny girl at the opposite end. But Daria reveled in the thrill of leaving shore behind, trailing her hand in the water, and being a thoroughly relaxed passenger. She even closed her eyes, feigning a nap, looking suddenly like the rosy incarnation of some Impressionistic painting I had seen somewhere. It was easy out in the middle of that lake to throw off all current concern, enter her land of make-believe, and pretend we really were father and daughter of another, simpler, calmer age.

The minnows are still in the pond, she reports, and the cat can't have eaten any more goldfish 'cause she counted them, and one of the baby tadpoles almost bumped into her finger. How do tadpoles become frogs? We talk about that for a while, lazily and not very scientifically, but Daria seems satisfied. She is touching the grey in my beard. "When I'm very, very old, like you, will I know everything and be able to stop asking everybody questions?"

I have exhausted my stock of replies to this tireless interrogator, this energetic child of my mid years, this do-it-yourself grandchild who sits thoughtfully expecting prompt response. Can I tell her that the summer is one of discovery for me, too, and of growth? Or that discoveries are often harsh, and growth painful? She is blissfully unaware that her wise and certain father stands indecisive at a major crossroad, trying to assess the unfamiliar, treacherous paths ahead.

Like a retriever on point, Daria has tensed to a sound I do not immediately hear, the sound of older brothers and sisters returning home, restoring to her that special world of rivalry, imitation, laughter, tears, and play. She leaps from my chest and races across the patio toward noise, excitement, and another kind of learning.

MY FATHER would have been eighty years old today. How appropriate that his birthdate should fall in late July, when so much that he loved could be enjoyed—long walks at dawn in green city parks, fresh seafood from the Chesapeake, seasonal crab feasts with cases of ice-cold beer on sweltering days, neighborhood tavern-doors thrown wide with men sharing joy and sorrow over countless pints, hot nights on the scrubbed white stoops of lean row-houses, the air static with many languages of a polygot community fused with that strange dialect from which Mencken fashioned a new vocabulary, Baltimorese.

All of this was the whole world to my father, and he was one of the most prejudiced men I have ever known. Convinced that this way of life in his particular city was superior to anything else imaginable, he rarely moved outside self-imposed boundaries. A railroad man, he let his wife and children travel extensively, content to remain behind alone. Of Italian heritage, he had none of the language and little of the culture of his parents' birthplace, and no curiosity about it. What in the Mediterranean could possibly be better than the streets of Baltimore he knew so well? After all, hadn't the families of most of his peers fled a Europe impoverished, technologically ignorant, politically corrupt, and morally bankrupt?

July celebrates America's Independence, and my father was an unabashedly enthusiastic flag-waver. Bearer of a tongue-twisting Basque-Italian name, he condemned all countries but the United States. His favorite performer of all time was the star-spangled George M. Cohan. And, if you caught him with the drink in him, thinking he was unobserved, he wasn't bad at a soft-shoe routine while crooning "Yankee Doodle Dandy." He had tried, I had heard, a bit of vaudeville in his youth, and had a talent-scout's ear for singling out potentially famous vocalists. But here, too, he was prejudiced, ignoring most music other than popular ballads.

We locked horns before I was ten. And on many issues they remained locked most of our lives. He disliked my liberalism about

music, unable to understand how—if I agreed with him on the impor-
tance of the music of Broadway—I could tolerate outlandish jazz,
symphony, foreign opera, Negro spirituals, and the blues. He admitted
that the Blacks produced "natural" singers, but the admission always
carried with it the suggestion that there was something mysterious,
alien, and threatening about this fact. Born and raised on the Mason-
Dixon line, he was a loyal and conforming citizen of a country that
practiced discrimination from coast to coast, north and south.

No one could have persuaded my father that Blacks were more
American than he, they having been in this country longer than his
own family. He often seemed blinded to his origin, referring to friends
of European descent as German-, Jewish-, Polish-, and Irish-
Americans, but thinking of himself in hyphenation only as red-white-
and-true-blue. When I resolved to go abroad for study, he seriously
tried to dissuade me, confounded by my interest in other lands and our
mutual ancestors. My excursions below Washington into the Deep
South provoked the comment that such places were racially imbal-
anced.

The last time I saw him was in an arena of pain at Johns Hopkins
Hospital, where he lay dying among other terminal patients in an in-
tensive-care unit. Disease had ravaged him, but death remained cruelly
elusive. Never before ill, always strong, furious at his own helplessness,
he glared at me with splendid wrath. Why didn't I put a weapon in his
hand, help him end the suffering? Why was I permitting the doctors to
keep him alive with machines? He couldn't speak to the women of the
family this way, but dammit, boy, you're a man and know men are not
machines.

The decision was not mine, and I tried to distract him—unsuccess-
fully, for he wanted no evasion of the facts at his deathbed. I noticed
how, strangely, I valued the shaft of anger directed against me. It was
the first in many years, for we had long ago drawn a truce ending the

fierce and bitter quarrels, the classic father-son confrontations bequeathed to us by Adam. We had settled into easy talk of grandchildren and gardening, over drinks casually shared. We had buried all hatchets. Now, as our hands locked and he hissed instructions I could not obey, I treasured the grit that so often in the past had triggered explosions between us.

His eyes turned soft, no longer on me but on someone moving beyond the foot of his bed. A young Black nurse was approaching us with a broad, defiant grin. Her ministrations to my father were exceedingly tender, but her words were roughly honed in the manner he understood. She gave him the gentlest care while somehow negating his complaints, flattering his manhood, and—though neither had ever heard of Dylan Thomas—feeding his rage against the dying light: Do Not Go Gentle into That Good Night.

He clearly worshipped her. It was painful to admit that a stranger could serve him better in these hours than relatives, priest, friends, or personal physician. But she was there, apparently whenever he needed her, while family visits were restricted in time. He said as much, believing himself abandoned by everyone but this beautiful Black woman in white.

After attending his needs, all the while bombarding him with affectionate banter, the nurse went off humming a blues song. My father's words were heartbreakingly poignant for a rough and unreflective man: "This damned corner is my world now—and that wonderful nigger is all I have in my world."

AUGUST

"Is it fiction," he pleaded, "that my sister,
after being raped, was nailed to a barn door and crucified?"

A LEG INJURY keeps me, highly impatient, flat on my back for too many hours each day. Years on the treadmill have ill-prepared me for inaction, and I chafe at the bit to be off and running. Bored with patterns on the ceiling, uninterested in most TV fare, too restless to read, I stare at the elevated leg or adjust heat-packs while swearing about work undone and piling up.

But one morning I resolve to accept my lot and simply sleep. But I have not slept late since I was a very young man, and my internal alarm clock respects no resolve. Each time my eyes open, I have to force them shut again; and in this manner I drift in and out of sleep through the morning.

The sun is warm, and our caged finches are chattering when I hear the two little girls singing in the patio. Live music (not recorded) is rare in our home, and I listen with keen interest. They are singing "Brother Sun, Sister Moon," a song they learned from a busload of out-of-state pilgrims with whom they traveled through Abiquiu and beyond to Christ in the Desert Monastery. I had been told that on the homeward trip the lurching bus resounded with community singing, and that the theme-tune from Zefferelli's movie was constantly repeated. The girls learned it note by note, word for word.

The finches—a red-eared waxbill and a tri-colored nun, both having distinctive calls—accompany the girls with enthusiasm. I rearrange the heat pack, recenter the leg on high pillows, close my eyes, and let the sound wash over me. Soon I am lost in a limbo not just between sleep and wakefulness, but in time.

When I was a boy, I woke to singing and birdsong every morning. Even before I opened my eyes in my bedroom over the kitchen, I would hear my mother's clear voice competing with a lusty canary and occasionally interrupted by the clatter of breakfast dishes. My mother sang all kinds of songs, new and old, of every nationality, and so sweetly that the neighbors of our city block threw open doors and windows to hear them—"Maria's singing!" Later in the day, one or two might ask the name of a melody they had particularly enjoyed.

Deaf in one ear, my mother was blessed with an unerring grace of tune in the other. Unable to read music, she was frequently called on by a semiprofessional pianist who played in movie houses and for social events. Whenever the woman had problems with unfamiliar music, she would invite my mother into her parlor, strike a few chords, and off they would go—the pianist struggling with the score in front of her, my mother warbling along in perfect pitch and harmony.

I hungered for a piano, but the depression of the Thirties ruled out luxuries in my family. My mother managed somehow to save fifteen dollars and purchased a battered old upright a neighbor wanted to be rid of. She handed me a self-instruction book, saying we could not afford formal lessons. When I learned to read notes and, clumsily, manage popular ballads, she was extremely proud—"he reads music!" —even though I had none of her natural musical gifts. Hard-saved pennies brought sheet music into the home, and I spent long hours after school laboring joyfully through sentimental favorites. My mother had no time to stand idly by me, but from wherever she was working in the house, she sang along as I played.

There are photos of her, hobble-skirted, corseted, with bobbed hair, linking arms with uniformed boys and laughing girls during World

War I. My father used to speak of her going into army canteens, sitting at the piano and playing every song the soldiers requested. "If you can hum it, I can play it." In those photos, though life had already treated her harshly, her smile is as glorious as any music I have ever heard.

She is white-haired now, not too well, a companion to illness and tragedy for many years. When I visit her, we share much conversation and camaraderie. I tease her about her habit of dozing off before the TV, not adding that in sleep all the pain in her life is exposed in a face bereft of its usual smile. Often, that's my last glimpse of her when I kiss her goodnight—dozing, remembering, holding to herself grief for the newest grave.

But in the morning, she is singing again. Irrepressible woman! Having waked first, and while busying myself in garden or basement, I hear her lovely song, still backed up by the clatter of breakfast dishes. When I come into her bright kitchen, she is as radiant as the sun in which she stands.

That sun has touched my pillow; it rouses me from the Chesapeake back to the Rio Grande. I need to stretch. Kicking aside heat packs, I hobble to the window and look below to the patio. The two little girls are bedding down their dolls under towels filched from Mommy's linen-shelf. They are still singing.

A FULL DAY of research at the University of New Mexico's music library ends with my remembering that I had promised Ellen to pick up two volumes of Camus she needs from the college bookstore. During the short walk across campus, I observe with much interest the hurrying young summer students; I feel alien in their world, a bit uncomfortable with their casual dress and undress, careless grooming and indifferent hygiene. It is better in the bookshop, where my generation fuses with theirs in a silent, serious perusal of the world's great literature. Art, once again the common denominator to men of all ages—or so I enjoy thinking.

Across the racks in front of me, a young woman sporting a short haircut is discussing Solzhenitsyn with a male escort tossing shoulder-length curls. They have recently read excerpts of *The Gulag Archipelago,* in translation, and the young man is arguing that the prisoner-of-war accounts "lack final credibility. They're superlatively written, of course, but the atrocities in them seem more literary than historic. Solzhenitsyn's a man who obviously loves words, language, and like so many great writers takes license to exaggerate, distort historical facts. We have to keep that in mind when reading his passionate, dramatic catalogue of terrors."

I study the couple with closer interest. The girl looks confused but is absently nodding agreement to her friend's thesis. They have dropped years in the past few seconds. I see them as children, hardly young adults; soft and petulant, untempered. The boy's casual sophistry closes an invisible wall between us, blots them from view. I turn my eyes to bright book-jacket designs, their patterns and colors suddenly whirling kaleidoscopically, radiating about a nimbus, wherein materializes the face of Stefan, with its familiar grin and mockery.

He was a Pole, not more than seventeen, short and thickset, with broad, rude features capped by a wild shock of yellow hair. I resented his being assigned to me, for sergeants did not rate orderlies, and I was accustomed to doing for myself. But our headquarters was employing, in those final weeks of the war, refugees of all nationalities who fought their way to the Colonel's desk and stubbornly demanded American sanctuary. The army had an instinct about the future need for such resourceful people once hostilities ended and Occupation began.

My quarters were luxurious for wartime, two small rooms that I had outfitted with appropriated furnishings, radio, books, an electric cooker, a stocked bar. Stefan's duties included policing the rooms, washing and ironing uniforms, shining boots, heating bath water. He did the work well and without a sense of servitude, but it was obviously a lark to him, a means toward richer gleanings. Too smart to steal and risk expulsion by the Americans, he never hesitated to ask for anything that caught his fancy. He accumulated a store of loot that was constantly being exchanged for essentials from the black market. Any meals he prepared for me or my friends included generous portions for the chef out of rations liberated from the mess hall. Stefan knew how to survive.

I had a hard time liking him. He talked incessantly, always with a wide grin that masked a terrifying barbarism. He had escaped both German and Russian refugee prison-camps, and he despised both nationalities. He was constantly advising me, or any American who could not escape his vitriol, not to end the war but to obliterate Germany, "men, women, and children, Nazi babies and all," and with that accomplished, roll on to annihilate, through arms and castration, all of Russia. On the eve of peace, he hungered for more bloodshed, total vengeance. After a while, my rooms seemed never free of his ravings. Or of a presence thoroughly malevolent, lurking behind the laughter of a teenaged boy.

Our orders to move out shattered him, and Stefan became morose. We were not taking him with us, so he had nothing to lose in turning light-fingered. Friends and I returned to the rooms one night to find him, sodden with schnapps he had pilfered, huddled in a corner in the dark. We jokingly tried to get him to bed. But for the first time, Stefan's horrible grin would not surface. He wept, crying that he loved us, that we were the only family he had now—where would he go and what would he do without us? Long exposure to his devious ways kept us cynically cool to these entreaties. He spoke of his parents, wailing about their persecution at the hands of all armies, allied and enemy. He piled atrocity on atrocity, describing the execution of mother and father by Russians as he watched from a nearby hideout in a clump of bushes. Again and again, he begged us not to abandon him.

One of our soldiers, cradling a glass of Cointreau, remarked that Stefan was an expert con-man; these histrionics were not to be taken seriously. With a wild cry, the young Pole jumped to his feet, threw himself with outstretched arms against a wall, and defied our disbelief.

"Is it fiction," he pleaded, "that my sister, after being raped, was nailed to a barn door and crucified? Didn't I see it? Is that what you're saying? Are those nails through the hands something I've only imagined? Is a lie driving me crazy?"

The silent embarrassment of the Americans hit him harder than physical blows would have. He slumped to the floor, whimpered himself to sleep, and we carried him to bed.

I have dropped one of the Camus books. Stooping to retrieve it, I see the young man and woman moving off down a bookstore aisle, heads together, still intently evaluating the poetic exaggerations of Alexander Solzhenitsyn. I resolve to read his *Archipelago*. Perhaps, in some small way, the book will help me live more peaceably with the memory of Stefan; will serve as in infinitesimal credit to a human debt that was fully acknowledged only too late and can never now be repaid.

THERE IS DANCING and feasting today at Santa Clara, honoring the patron saint for whom the pueblo is named. My family will most likely go among the people, as we did last year, to share their beautiful chants and dances, delicious food, and gracious hospitality. It is fitting

—with our strong emotional ties to Umbria and New Mexico—that we join in celebration and devotions for the Lady of Assisi along the banks of the Rio Grande.

Chiara went with us to the pueblo on her name-day last year, and I saw in her eyes the same questioning she experienced at Assisi: "Who and what was this woman whose name I bear; why, when she's never mentioned among my friends and schoolmates, is such a fuss made in a remote Italian hilltown or the dusty plaza of a southwest pueblo?" Through travel and interests nomenclatural, we have bequeathed our daughter a curiosity and pride in her namesake, which promises to grow, in interest and study, throughout her life.

The child's name was chosen fourteen years before her birth, when her mother, on a postgraduate study-tour of Europe, stood in the basilica of Santa Chiara and vowed she would have a daughter called Chiara. It is a name not commonly used, even in Italy, where the word, uncapitalized, is most frequently employed as an adjective. In that sense too, meaning bright or clear—clarity—it is an apt name for our second daughter.

Chiara was not yet five when she first journeyed with us to Assisi. Almost immediately, education about her patron saint was under way, for our first action in the town was to bang on the barred gates at the convent of the Poor Clares. We had heard that they accepted guests at much lower rates than the hotels. An elderly nun opened the gate, babbling in French, rather surprised at the large family (with infant yet, *Mon Dieu!*), and concerned that we have proper accommodations. Preoccupied with household tasks, impatient with our rusty French and lapses into Italian (which she did not understand), she brusquely hurried us toward very comfortable quarters. Only when we were settled did the nun relax and look carefully at each of us. She was delighted to find, among our crowd, two of the reasons for which we had come to Assisi—daughters named Pier Francesca and Chiara. *"Francoise et Claire—bien nommées."*

The convent, beautifully restored in the architectural tradition of the town, was a serene island of France in the heart of Italy. All the guests except for us were French; the meals were French; even the thought—I felt—was French. Because we were American, because the five children ranged in age from sixteen years down to two months, because we could not be ignored, we received extravagant attention from the nuns and the other guests. Chiara grew accustomed to strangers' putting a hand on her head, commenting that this was the child named for Clare. She saw in the convent's contemporary chapel, in the dining room, and on the wall of her own room, the finest representations of the saint—the mother superior of the Poor Clares had a discerning eye in art. Chiara began to identify with the beautiful lady in the paintings.

There is much to see in Assisi, but unfortunately we had little time. We were not always certain as to where the older children were wandering after personal interests. Chiara, intimidated by crowds of pilgrims, held on to her parents' hands. But often, absorbed in the great shrines, art masterpieces, and, especially, the mystical atmosphere that even today permeates Assisi, I forgot the wide-eyed child was at my side. In the basilica of Santa Chiara, which the little girl had by now embraced as something particularly hers, we made the mistake of not checking out all exhibits in advance.

Among them is the glass-encased body of Santa Chiara. It is extremely well preserved for a woman of the twelfth century. But to a child of five it came as a great shock—the dark coloring of the flesh, especially, unnerved Chiara. We had unwittingly robbed her of the lovely image in her mind.

The Giottos and the Cimabues helped restore that image. We pointed out to the child every appearance of Clare in the frescos. At the souvenir shop, we purchased miniature reproductions of the saint's portrait, as well as handsome books featuring her in full-color plates. Older brothers and sister instructed Chiara in elementary lessons of time and decay, steering her out of crypts and toward the light. Within a day, the specter began to recede.

Chiara met a young woman named Clare last August, and they resolved to do something special on their feastday. Clare is a talented dancer and obtained permission from her priest to present an offertory dance at the commemorative Mass. For one full afternoon, she instructed Chiara in simple liturgical body-movement. Their dance, lasting but a few minutes, was a free and joyous celebration, the woman and child moving together in great beauty. Chiara is a naturally shy girl, but this public act of reverence betrayed no self-consciousness. Rather, her face was aglow with wondrous light, as bright and clear and shining as the name she bears.

SEPTEMBER

"Of course, she suffered—
grievously, monstrously."

WANTING a guarantee for an early rising, I had plugged the bedroom television set into an automatic timer. If anything could drive me out of bed after a late night, the tube was it. Now, as snatches of newscasts and celebrity interviews buffet me relentlessly toward consciousness, I have nothing but regret. What a helluva way to surrender the balm of sleep, to begin any day.

Silken dreams of sunny shores displaced by weather reports of an incoming cold front; fantasies of privileged leisure blown away by the latest threats of government collapse and more austerity. Peering over the blanket's edge, I can see pink lips rhythmically mouthing doomsday across the black room: emergency sessions in Washington and at the United Nations, retail prices up, Wall Street down, late statistics of weekend traffic fatalities, there's been another high defection in the Catholic Church, one of our millionaires is missing, the Supreme Court's bogged down on a pornography ruling, and Hazel Hollywood has found a new Great and Good Friend though the fifth divorce is not yet final!

I almost regain paradise during a mattress commercial denouncing morning backache. Morpheus has me by the hand, has sealed off audio pollution, has lowered my eyelids, and is drawing me into an underworld miraculously free of technology. We are in a landscape fashioned of art supplies, easels and gigantic brushes piercing the air like skyscrapers; and of completed projects, canvases, bronzes, and manuscripts punctuating the perspective *à la* De Chirico's or Dali's surrealisms. There are no clocks, alarmed or otherwise. It is a place of endless hours, with all the tools of one's choice of work at hand. The only other creatures are idealized nymphs, at a good distance, awaiting one's time and pleasure.

But Morpheus deserts me, the bubble bursts, and the mattress commercial concludes with a head-rattling crescendo. I sit bolt-upright in bed, blearily watching a reclining model (without backache) do a slow dissolve into this morning's special guest, a young woman from Oregon promoting her just-published, on-your-newsstands-today clinical study of the Sexual Revolution and the dissolution of the Marriage Ethic. Without a remote control to turn the set off, dreading the chill outside the blankets and still not fully awake, I hunch captive at the head of the bed, mesmerized by an electronic Instant-Psychologist so pitifully out of reach against that far, far wall.

The Insular Family's anachronistic, I am assured by the Bright Young Person, and so are—"really, it's just not relevant anymore"—the pretensions of husband, father, provider and protector, breadwinner. Why did I hook up this monster to an automatic timer, anyway, if the day's tight schedule need not be met, if financial commitments need not be honored? The New Freedom has liberated us all (the voice purrs on) from traditional roles (and responsibilities?), with Unisex permitting us the widest choice and range of behavior. If Zero Population Growth were respected (where can I stash those five kids conceived and born before ZPG existed?), all the institutional and social demands made on Persons as husband-wife, father-mother would simply disappear.

She's fairly young, the television hostess suggests; is the book based on experience? Well, yes. Though under thirty, our writer-of-the-day has three failed marriages—"but friendly divorces"—behind her, so her thesis is not entirely theoretical. Her face tautens for only a second before the toothpaste smile flashes again. At present she has a Relationship with someone with whom she can be Soft and Tender minus the burden of Contractual Inanities. She hopes—hurriedly, with twenty seconds till signoff—that the book will enjoy wide popularity, not only for the royalties, "though one must live," but because she truly believes it has Something Important to say to the Youth of America. That does it: I'm out of bed, across the room, and the set is off.

But the adrenalin is not exactly surging as I fumble at the kitchen light switch and rattle dishes in a sleepy-eyed grab for the coffeepot. The illuminated dial of the range clock nags that I'd better get a move on, the dawn will soon be up heralding a bright new day crammed with all the hassles of earning a living. The cat has leaped on the counter, meowing and brushing my elbow, demanding her daily bread. The dog sits at my feet, her sad eyes reproaching me for keeping her waiting to be let outdoors. Our noise has wakened Daria, who comes from her room in tears, has no idea where she is, what's wrong, or what she wants, and cannot be comforted. I kneel on the floor, take her in my arms and drown in a sea of bawling child, mewing cat, and whimpering dog.

They all want to be served. None of them heard that TV show or know anything at all about the New Freedom.

DON LORENZO was skipping church again. I came across him in one of the villa's field-sheds, where he was solemnly sorting apples, setting aside the finest from his orchard for fermentation to brandy. His hounds lay at his feet, and the door and windows of the rude shelter were thrown wide to admit a bracing mid-September breeze.

The pealing of church bells sounded over our greeting. Don Lorenzo favored me with a conspiratorial smile.

"But of course you're American," he said, "and these feastdays so important to we Tuscani can't mean much in your country. Even so, as a guest, you should have joined my wife and daughters, and my son, in the procession. Now they'll consider you an iconoclast, as they do me."

"The Mater Dolorosa is not much venerated in the United States except in our Southwest. There she's known as Nuestra Señora de los Dolores."

"*Bien nommé*. I've seen some of her images in Spain. They are frequently as bad as our own. I hope that your instructors at the Accademia—if anyone is even remotedly interested in religious art these days—caution you against sentimental abuses in representations of Santa Maria."

"The subject never comes up."

"Of course not. There's a worldwide conspiracy, you know, which claims that *any* picture or carving of the madonna is intrinsically good and therefore exempt from criticism. What rot. Rarely have artists portrayed her with all the passion, dignity, strength, and individuality which she unquestionably has as the mother of God; and which is so manifest in scripture, in every historical word we have of her. The Teutonics present her too often as harsh and brooding, frigid; the French made her a fashionable lady; the Spanish give us gloomy duennas. But leave it to *noi Italiani* to commit the gravest sins against her —artists of the Renaissance painting their mistresses with golden halos and folded hands, titling those spoiled, petulant, sometimes stupid creatures 'Maria.' *Disgraciata!*"

"But I disagree. Valid iconography does exist."

"Certainly. Mankind's not entirely graceless—occasionally we manage a Rembrandt, a Michelangelo, an El Greco, or a Murillo. Even, in our times, a Rouault. But for every sublime vision of men like these, we have hundreds, thousands of weak, insipid, sanctimonious paintings and sculptures, plaster casts and gaudy prints of a false Maria. And those, *amico mio,* because they're often inexpensive, are what's grabbed up by the deluded masses."

"What do you want in portrayals of the Virgin?"

"I'll tell you what I don't want," Don Lorenzo retorted. "What my family's now carrying in procession—the statue of a self-pitying woman, tearful eyes rolled heavenward, sweet lips primly pursed in pious forebearance, dressed in freshly starched petticoats and the finest black damask, lace-trimmed! Oh, I don't deny that preparation of her garments gives our local signoras a worthwhile task and keeps them from harmful mischief. But how much better if they robed her more simply, honestly, more like a woman of the ancient Holy Land.

"And if the carver had meditated, thought even a little about what she must have been. Maria was no romantic but an exceptional Jewess, married under controversial circumstances, mother of a Messiah branded Radical and Revolutionary by most of their contemporaries. Her obedience to the will of God is for me no meek cowering but a supreme act of courage. Read of her behavior at Bethlehem; with her twelve-year-old in the temple; at Cana; in the midst of rough, frightened men at Pentecost. Here was a woman, tough, gentle, made of steel; here, always, was strength."

"Yes. But that is only one aspect of a very complex individual who's become many different things to a diverse humanity. The Dolorosas present another side of her."

"I protest. Of course she suffered—grievously, monstrously. Exclusively, I believe, because she was chosen for, and accepted, anguish never before or since granted any mortal. The sword through the heart is a valid symbol; but representations which limit her to grief cheat us. Think of the joy she must have known in the divinity of her Son; of her boldness in facing criticism from conventional peers with less controversial children; of how independent and resolute she must have been while never challenging civil or religious authority and tradition.

All this coupled with a compassion and tenderness we find evident in every scriptural mention of her. Here was an extraordinary human being, the Utopian ideal we seek in the twentieth century, that embodiment of human perfection which overcomes all qualifications of race, creed, and gender, of nationality. Here was man as he can be, in total dignity. That's what I want, though rarely find, in representations of Maria."

Don Lorenzo said these things long before our present concerns about racial, sexual, and political liberations became fashionable. For many years, his words influenced me to study too critically and often with cynicism the myriad attempts of artists to capture the spirit of Mary in paint or stone. More often than not, I had to admit that he was right, that painter and sculptor repeatedly demeaned the Virgin by imposing on her their personal sentimentalities about femininity, sweetness, beauty, and submission—and at their worst, glamorizing her into a cosmetically celestial creature competitive with the shimmering stars of Hollywood.

But that was before I came to New Mexico and saw for the first time the carvings of Nuestra Señora de los Dolores produced by native santeros. There is nothing false in this iconography. Everything that Don Lorenzo asked for is in these proud yet humble images. The santeros, in most cases not so educated or sophisticated as my Tuscan friend, not able to verbalize the qualities of Maria as he did, have expressed the selfsame thing through their handicraft. For behind the obvious sorrows in the bultos and retablos of our numerous Dolores are the particular strengths, virtues, and universality that men of faith have always found in the Blessed among women.

On this her feast day I shall visit the Museum of International Folk Art or perhaps a Santa Fe church and look again on one of those powerful, reverent works of our inspired santeros—a carving of Nuestra Señora de los Dolores.

THE WAITRESS brings plates burdened with enchiladas, tacos, and tamales. The boy has always favored regional cooking, but he eats now with unusual gusto. Perhaps, I think, in anticipation of the return to a campus diningroom with its bland menus. Better stoke up while he can.

We are in a café at the edge of town, a few miles from his dormitory, where we have just unloaded gear and paraphernalia he had brought home for the holiday. I can see, through a cheaply curtained window, the desert stretching flat and arid, butting abruptly in the northwest against the base of the Magdalenas. The Penitent Woman on her back, formed by those amazing crests against the skyline, is barely discernible from here. But I know she is there.

We are comfortable with each other, not forcing conversation and mercifully free of father-son conventions. When, I wonder (for I cannot remember), did we abandon the father-child relationship and begin to know each other as individuals outside the family hierarchy?

Easy talk leads slowly and without passion to his amused consideration of a possible change of career-plans in this, his final year of college. He has wanted oceanology since he was very small, that ambition never before wavering. His mother and I watched for many years, with interest and respect, his single-mindedness in matters scientific and especially in everything pertinent to marine life. We have spent a great deal of time near or on the sea as a family, swimming beside him off both coasts of the United States, along Mexican shores, and in the Mediterranean. Once we detoured many miles around landslides and horrendous traffic jams on the Riviera to get him to Monaco's famed Oceanographic Institute. He introduced us to the joys of skin-diving and the aquatic underworld at Taormina. We have visited countless celebrated aquariums with him, known his personal generations of fish and much of the research and pleasure he has gleaned from them. He has gifted his parents, brothers, and sisters with a share in that pleasure and knowledge, opening windows for each of us to the wonders and promise of the riches of the sea.

All of our children are talented in the arts but utterly realistic about them. They have lived too closely with the inherent sacrifices, to hold any romantic notions about the creative professions. Gian's scientific papers and reports were frequently enhanced by superb drawings and illustrations, and he was content to have this graphic facility play a supporting role to his major study. At college, he has earned money by working in stage lighting, at which he has done a superior job, aided by fascination with electronics, his sense of design, and the technology of rock concerts, light shows, and modern theater. Advisors have suggested that he is too gifted in the theater arts to slight them. An associate has left school and is working Off-Broadway, urges him to follow suit. A girl in the picture is a fine-arts major.

Gian tells me of his change of heart with, I suspect, deliberate casualness. I feel a pang of apprehension—will I have to behave and sound like a parent? When I don't want to? When it's so much easier and pleasanter simply to share man-talk over a good dinner? God forbid that I push the children down reluctant paths. He is our first-born, and in these unfamiliar waters I find myself treading cautiously.

But, fortunately, we stay afloat, not denying familial concern and accountability, but refusing to let personal freedoms be abused. Gian nods smilingly at my litany of horrors in the art world. I say only a fraction of what is coursing through my mind, remembering his mother's imaginative work in stage design, all those unemployed, hungry actors we knew in Woodstock and the Village; remembering lean student days, painters fainting at easels from lack of breakfast (and, often, lunch and dinner); aching with the experience of energies expended on every canvas, sculpture, manuscript, mosaic, or relief; mindful of cutbacks made on table, wardrobe, and furnishings because artists need and want—require—costly books and music, supplies and materials, museum fees and theater tickets, concert admissions, and, perhaps the biggest dent in the pocketbook, travel—that gateway to peoples and cultures and the knowledge necessary to interpret them.

All the slights of philistines who fear what is different, all the haggling over fees and contracts with an American clientele too long convinced that Art is a dilettantish avocation, not a demanding profession to be as scrupulously reimbursed as those of doctor, lawyer, Indian chief. All the perpetual torments and endless labors.

I have not said it all, and do not need to. Gian is well aware that the frequent, anguished complaints have never killed my love of the arts, nor tempered in any way his mother's and my total compulsion for and commitment to them. He values the stimulation of our diverse, original, and creative friends, the daring and adventure of many of our underbudgeted but farflung travels, a home where family passions and conflicts revolve more often around ideas and philosophies than around possessions or diversions. He is grinning and (I tell myself) not seriously troubled at any threat to his first love, oceanology. "I know," he says, "I know all about how tough it is in the arts. But gee—dammit, Dad, you just can't beat the lifestyle!"

I am surprisingly flattered, and moved, and anxious to repeat his evaluation to his mother.

WE WERE RETURNING in a weapons carrier from a supply detail that had taken us into Kassel. The September sun was warm, and we had stripped off fatigue jackets, letting the heat penetrate bare, sore muscles. Most of the men sprawled against dufflebags in the open rumbling truck, fighting boredom, exhaustion, or despair with sleep. I sat upright once we were free of the ruined city, marveling at the green fields rolling away from each side of the ribboned autobahn, delighting in the profusion of wild flowers. The countryside was fresh, clean, and verdant; and sometimes for miles one saw no evidence, no trace, of the recent holocaust.

Perhaps, however, my companions with the tightly closed eyes chose the wiser course. For one could not really escape the devastation, and each approach to small towns brought the usual tableau of wrecked, rusting machinery, pocked farmlands, gaping barns and houses. Every railroad crossing revealed the blasted tracks, twisted strips of metal forming grotesque compositions, frequently like the uplifted, pleading arms of an abstract sculpture against impersonal skies. Starving men and women glowered from within the hollow shells of what had been their homes. Emaciated children flung themselves at our truck. Ears remained closed against their cries of *"Ich habe hunger"* as defiantly as eyes remained sealed against their gaunt skulls and wasted limbs.

An old dogface, sharing my meal of tinned rations, explained why he slept, or feigned sleep, whenever on these details. "I've come through the war with my life; I want to go home with my sanity. That means I must see, hear, feel as little as possible. Once I believed nothing could be worse than war. I was wrong—a country in defeat is."

We entered Eschwege and stopped before the neat cluster of suburban buildings that served as battalion headquarters. The area was incongruously unblemished, a bourgeois neighborhood boasting tree-lined, symmetrical streets, lawns and gardens, houses whose owners had once taken pride in maintenance. But the porch and front steps of our administration offices were jammed with human flotsam, unemployed townsfolk seeking work, refugees from other nations demanding asylum, released prisoners of war with nowhere to go and wanting renewed incarceration or transportation home. We were an anti-aircraft unit, unequipped and unauthorized to deal with these people. And though we had posted numerous signs, and reiterated verbally every day that they take their problems to Military Government, their ranks never dwindled. Whenever we left our beds, from our first waking moment, their eyes burned into us, and their hands reached out voraciously.

From our position in the weapons carrier, the old dogface swore: "God, I don't think I can take much more of them. The war's over;

why can't they leave us alone.'' Beyond him, I could see our own personnel being accosted by the alien, anxious hands, deafened by the curses of foreign tongues. Men I had lived with for three years and found resolute in combat were now cracking under the strain of human demands for which they had no resources and no answers.

My eyes incautiously lingered on two blond children, a boy and a girl, near the trash cans outside our mess hall. The little girl had wolfed down garbage too greedily and was now tearfully retching, while her brother supported her spasmed body. Morning-glories cascaded brilliantly on a fence behind them. Like that shower of blossoms, something exploded inside me. I lowered myself from the truck and walked away from the houses, out of Eschwege, turning my back on everything there.

Flight was easy, accomplished by hitching rides on military vehicles. The drivers asked no questions. I fled, without conscious thought or plan, to a distant spa I had never before visited, but where, I knew, Clare was stationed. We had long shared a camaraderie founded on the instinct for survival, mental as well as physical. I would remain absent without leave—for the first time—so long as necessary for subtle wounds to heal.

The spa was a bright garden of a town surrounded by dense forests in the foothills of a luxuriant range. Its sanitariums, thermal baths, watering pavilions, inns, and casinos were flanked by narrow, hilly streets graced with storybook gingerbread houses. I entered the community with the elated sense of a civilian tourist come in peacetime for the waters and a cure.

But the deception was immediately vanquished. The spa now served as a hospital-town for wounded soldiers from the Wehrmacht. The crippled and lame, the bandaged, the blind and the senseless, men without an arm or a leg, the paraplegics—walked, hobbled, or were wheeled out of the once fashionable sanitariums into all the sunny, September-flowered streets and lanes. Seeing an American, their hands immediately went out—for a bar of chocolate, a cigarette, would you possibly have schnapps in that canteen. My meager hoardings were instantly depleted.

I slowly became aware of hausfraus, aproned, standing in their doorways. Arms crossed, stern of visage, they leaned silently against jambs, watching their maimed countrymen's painful procession under the sparking sun. Their eyes were hard with loathing, which I assumed was directed against me. But a paralyzed veteran, wheeled to my side by a nurse and denied a cigarette because I had none to give him, ruthlessly put me straight.

"Their hatred is not for you, the victor; but for us, the defeated. We lost their war, their livelihoods, their security. This town once prospered on moneyed tourists; now it is crawling with casualties."

I resisted his brutal explanation. But only a few steps farther on, I heard a woman hiss at a wounded youth and saw her spit at his feet before slamming the door against his piteous scars.

I found Clare in a tented bivouac-area, where he was on communications duty. He had not moved from his bunk, a sergeant informed me, for two days. He was not ill but lay with a blanket drawn over his head. He acknowledged my arrival with a grunt but refused to get up. I poured cognac from a half-emptied bottle and tried to cajole him into conversation, remarking on the beautiful day, the need to rise and shine, seek diversion, a bit of carousing or debauchery. Eventually he lowered the blanket from his face and stared at me with hollowed, red-rimmed eyes. "Have you taken a good long look at this town?" Then he retreated once more into his world of darkness, and I sat silently, sipping the cognac.

OCTOBER

"Never believe I am dead until you
see my body covered with cloth of gold."

I AM ALONE in the rectory, with blueprints of the adjacent building spread wide on a dining table. The task seems monumental—renovation of a structure originally designed as a gymnasium, later used as a temporary chapel, finally to be a contemporary church, which may or may not one day be designated a cathedral. My head is heavy with architectural dimensions, specifications; the sketches under my hand, blurring before my eyes, persuade me that I've earned a pre-luncheon scotch. I pour a drink and peruse the absent host's collection of recorded music. Eileen Farrell fills the room with arias from *Turandot*.

I am in the Texas panhandle. From a glass wall I look out over plains stretching from horizon to horizon, the sky low and flat above barely perceptible squat houses and institutional buildings. This complex of church properties sits at the edge of a mushrooming southwestern city; the rectory is an attractive, comfortable, civilized hostel during my brief sojourn out of the mountains. For the hundredth time, squinting uneasily at limitless vistas, to that point where earth melds into sky, I think of the Sangres and know I have become a man of the mountains—as once I was, and always will be, a man of the seas.

But the plains of West Texas hold a surprising and undeniable attraction. I am tempted to climb high, scale a tower or silo as I had climbed the masts of ships, and command a 360-degree view of the vast land. I leave the rectory, blueprints under one arm, and tramp across deserted athletic fields in order to put distance between myself and the church, to get a better perspective of its bulk rising solidly from the earth. The skies have gone yellow, not unlike the brick of the building, and everything under the sun seems drained of true color, minuscule, terrifyingly small and unimportant. What value my work or the labors of priest associates with whom I have spent these past few days—what value any of man's efforts—against these impersonal, intimidating, boundless heavens?

A cold wind rises, biting my flesh, tearing at clothing and the gear I carry. My footsteps flush a jackrabbit, the largest I have ever seen. It leaps a short distance away, then takes a stand and glares at me, the intruder in its territory. Even here, where land appears to stretch to infinity, man and beast compete for a bit of breathing space. When I resume walking, the rabbit's eyes bulge with mortal fear before it takes swift flight, bouncing across the wide fields in graceful arcs until lost in the far distance.

Back at the rectory, I pick up the abandoned scotch and start again the disc of *Turandot*. Something has been nagging at me, some vague cynicism about work and effort, some seductive call toward idleness and noncommitment. Neither the scotch nor Puccini are of much help. Has working alone amid these enormous stretches of relentless earth and sky brought this on? Not entirely. On all sides are the tools and evidence of my host's profession and interests; his books and worksheets, parish schedules, lists of community activities. He belongs to a people whom he serves day and night—I have seen them at his door, heard the persistent phone-calls, witnessed his solicitude and counseling to others while driving himself on a hard, lonely road of self-denial. His hospitality and attention to my needs have been not only generous but presented with obvious recognition that I am someone special, his beloved brother in Christ, a child of God. Knowing my own unworthiness, I have, I perceive, been questioning the value of all sacrifice and work.

A stranger enters the room, and we introduce ourselves. He is from an outlying parish, in town for the day, an FBI (foreign-born Irish) who needs to use the phone. He has just learned that a child from his parochial school was struck by a car on her way home for lunch, and wishes to call the hospital. He looks very tired, near exhaustion; the morning has been crowded with taxing business—and now this. I listen to a native brogue strangely laced with Texan accent as he labors away at the phone, trying to get information about his small parishioner. Eventually, he is speaking to the child's father; and the injuries— "praise the Lord"—are not fatal and do not appear to be too serious. I return to the glass wall and those endless plains and deliberately screen out the priest's soft, gentle words of consolation. I am stuck now, perhaps for so long as I live, with the image of a young parent I have never seen, in pain and terror and grief. And also with that bent, weary figure of a spent man in dogged ministry.

I WENT AGAIN and again on weekends through the school year to Franco's parents' country home, even when he was not there, when studies forced him to remain at the university in Modena. Once, I found the villa deserted by all members of the large family except his mother, living here now on a permanent basis. She formally offered me hospitality and opportunity for respite from the city, for renewal on this Tuscan farm; then she quietly withdrew. The main house was elegantly rustic, my room spare and isolated; and I was free from all social obligation. La Signora valued her privacy as much as I. We contrived to avoid one another.

The land was my greatest joy. Rising at the crack of dawn, I would wander hill and dale across fields incredibly cultivated, compositioned

like the painted landscapes I was studying at Firenze. The local farm-
ers used terracing, hedgerows, and cypress in a manner astoundingly
similar to that observed in the stylized backgrounds of Renaissance
masterpieces. There were uneasy moments in the still mornings before
the pearly mists had lifted, moments when I was not quite sure
whether I was awake or dreaming, whether I was really in the country
or had been beguiled, seduced, and drawn into the surrealistic vortex
of pigmentation and canvas.

The dreamlike ambiance persisted when I returned to the house.
Accustomed to the loud activities of Franco and his sisters in those
stark rooms, or to the musings of his father, Don Lorenzo, over shared
blessings from their vineyard, I experienced a sense of acute alienation
among once-familiar surroundings. This feeling was less the result of
being alone—for I had grown accustomed to that, and perhaps preferred it to company; I was frequently accused of being a loner, and I
had come to this house to escape the teeming streets of Florence—than
of not being alone, of being constantly aware of La Signora. She
seemed always to be one step ahead of me, appearing and disappearing
at the edge of my vision, almost as though whenever I entered her
home, I had disturbed her at something and caused her to move on.
Once, approaching the library for a book, I thought I heard her sobbing behind the closed door.

We did not dine together, but ample fare was on the diningroom
sideboard whenever I wanted it. The cook, whom I appreciated well
from previous visits, was not on the premises. Signora did not bother
with hot meals. Fruits, breads, cheeses, nuts, and wine sufficed while
her family was away. I knew Don Lorenzo's business interests kept
him in the city a great deal (he preferred it that way) and that Franco
and an elder sister elected to spend most of the school vacations in their
university towns. I had heard a rumor that another of the girls had run
off to Rome with a foreign student. But there were three other teenaged daughters, and the house had always echoed with their boister-
ousness, as well as with the comings and goings of many family

friends. Only now, during this stilled weekend, did I recognize that none of those visitors had ever arrived expressly to see Signora. They were all, like myself, friends of her husband or children. Did they all, like myself, tend to ignore the beautiful woman who sat quietly smiling in the background while passion roared through her house?

Don Lorenzo, his son and daughters—and most of their friends—were expansive, volatile people; sensual, given to food and drink and continuous debate in half a dozen languages on the humanities and the arts, politics, philosophy, and the eternal perplexities of man. Now I remembered that Signora had never joined any of these discussions—that she had probably tolerated all of us, waiting for us to be gone, waiting to reclaim the house to herself.

On Sunday noon, I hiked into the village. There were a few curious paintings in the local church and a rather handsome, though small, stone fountain in the piazza that fronted it. I told myself that I wanted to sketch, but perhaps Signora's quiet presence had driven me from the house. I was not surprised when a casual acquaintance, a friend of the Don's, stopped me to ask—with concerned curiosity—how she was. I made some noncommittal response about her well-being. The man shook his head.

"She's lost them all, hasn't she—even the youngest children away to schools now. What ails our lovely lady?"

I returned to the farm in late afternoon to pick up my small grip before boarding the last bus for Florence. Wanting to say farewell to the Signora—we had exchanged no word since our greeting two days earlier—I was surprised that she was, suddenly, nowhere to be seen or overheard. I walked through the rooms of the house, out to the sheds, and scanned the fields. When I could delay no longer, I ran to the road where the bus was already approaching its stop-point. The vehicle was crowded, and I elbowed my way toward the rear, prepared for a long stand back to the city. Bending down to anchor my pack under a seat, I happened to glance out the window. The Signora was standing by a roadside shrine, looking directly at me, and she was weeping.

MY ATTENTION strays from the immediate boundaries of a map I am preparing of New Mexico's Rio Grand Underground Water Basin. The southern boundary ends the Basin just below Elephant Butte Reservoir, but my eye continues down a detailed Geological Survey chart following the Rio into Doña Ana County and the Mesilla Valley. Countless visits to this area of the state have made me familiar with the fertile fields flanking the river, the arid plains dotted with mesas, the lofty peaks of the Organs. And here on the map, outlined in standard cartographic symbol, is the old Santa Teresa land-grant, poised just above the border, before the Rio plunges into Texas and Old Mexico.

Teresa is not a common place-name in New Mexico, and I find it appropriate that the grant is as close as one can get in the state to Central and South America. It reminds me that all of St. Teresa's brothers joined Spanish expeditions to the New World, in Peru and on the Rio de la Plata and in Ecuador, where her favorite brother, Lorenzo, amassed a fortune and contributed heavily to her work as a Foundress in Spain.

Tomorrow is Teresa of Avila's feastday; and in the streets of her birthplace, fiesta has been under way for a week. Except for Spain (and at the Vatican), the day, for the most part, will go unobserved through the rest of the world. Teresa is not an "easy" saint, not one to romanticize or sentimentalize, and today's Christians largely ignore her. Yet this sixteenth-century enigmatic reformer of the Carmelites had much in common with modern man. Frivolous and worldly as a young, beautiful, sensuous noblewoman, self-destructive, she suffered many ills we consider peculiarly contemporary—spiritual confusion, depression, nervous breakdown, gastric disorders, tension headaches, even the problem of an increasing girth with advancing age. Many of our quick-remedy television commercials, fad diets, and quack-therapy ads might have been directed at St. Teresa. The beauty of her life was that all these familiar, tiresome, and debilitating mental and physical onslaughts never destroyed her. Again and again in her life, punch-drunk, she literally picked herself up off the floor, faced the newest challenge, and went out to meet it.

Biographies of Teresa are plentiful, but none are better than her renowned autobiographical works, *Life* and *The Interior Castle*. Her life is so well documented that there has been little chance for legends to take root. I have heard a modern one about her appearance as an old woman before the walls of Avila during the Spanish Civil War. When the Republican army, not knowing how well the city was defended, questioned the old woman about Nationalist troops inside the walls, she led them to believe the town was strongly fortified. The Republicans retired, and Avila escaped untouched, though it was practically undefended and could have been obliterated.

More interesting, and mystifying, are the eyewitness accounts we have of her life. During her early twenties she became severely ill following inexpert medical and spiritual counsel after a nervous collapse. Brought to her father's home to die, she quickly passed into unconsciousness and was administered the last rites. A mirror was held to her face, and no sign of breath appeared on it. Hot wax from a candle, used for a close examination, fell and sealed her eyelids, which did not flutter. Another candle, unattended by her drowsy brother Lorenzo, who was keeping vigil, set fire to the draperies, causing havoc until they were extinguished. Nuns washed and shrouded the body, but Teresa's father would not surrender her to the grave. He remained at her side, his fingers on her wrist, hoping to feel a pulse.

After four days, Teresa's hand moved along her shroud and the fingers removed the wax from her sealed eyelids. To her astounded father, she spoke with authority and prophecy—if cryptically—of the work she must do in this world: "Never believe I am dead until you see my body covered with cloth of gold."

As an old woman famous throughout Spain for the convents she had founded, for her writings and her intellectual gifts to the Church, she was summoned by the Duchess of Alba to be present at the birth of a grandson and heir. Teresa, tired and feverish after a strenuous journey, and learning that the baby was born before she could arrive, spent the night at Alba in one of her convents rather than at the palace. Here she died, and for the second time in her long years, nuns washed and shrouded the body. The wealthy and the royal, princes of state from government and Church, were hurrying from all over Spain to attend the funeral. But the nuns clothed Teresa—as they knew she would have insisted—in her threadbare habit and veil. Then they assisted workmen excavating a place for the coffin in the chapel's masonry.

All was attended to when the Duchess of Alba arrived and stepped forward to place a pall over the simple bier. It was a magnificent length of cloth of gold.

I know a priest who feels great affinity with Teresa of Avila. He shares many of the quarrels she had against the institutional Church and its intrigues. Outspoken and frequently impolitic, as she could be, he has shocked pious Christians by downgrading some of their cherished "sweeter" saints in favor of the harsher Teresa. She may be, he tells me, finally winning some devotion from modern man. She has been elected—by his vote or the ladies', I do not know—patroness of the Feminist Movement.

I HAVE BEEN balancing books, when one of the children rings the dinner-bell. Pencil poised midway over a long column of figures, I see, without completing the addition, that the total will be disappointing. Once again, inflation is eating us alive. Where to trim, where to prune expenses already cut to essentials? As if throwing salt on a wound, a radio news-commentator is reporting the latest rise in the national cost-of-living index. Rather abruptly, I turn the dial, shutting out the sound before going in to dinner.

We are barely seated at the table when Daria upsets her glass of milk. I watch the creamy liquid swirl between plates and glasses, course to the edge of the table, and cascade to the floor. Brother and sister are blotting the standing pools with paper napkins; mother has reached for a sponge. A family effort is under way to restore order and proceed with the meal. I alone am motionless, staring at a few collected drops of milk near my foot, thinking budgets and waste and high-spirited four-year-olds. I am thinking also of something else, something nudging my memory, drawing me into a landscape as white and colorless as the milk itself. Something. . . .

Of course. The fields, flat and endless, were robbed of all color by heavy snow and leaden skies. Our vehicles had labored over the icy roads for two days, skirting frozen, upended livestock whose stiffened limbs pointed accusingly at merciless heavens. The region was stripped of firewood, and no smoke rose from the chimneys of isolated farmhouses, badly shelled or otherwise violated. From these hovels, gaunt women and children sometimes emerged, staring expressionless at our mechanized convoy. They, and we, were too numbed by cold and hunger to attempt a greeting or any other human gesture.

A quartermaster fiasco at the last supply depot had issued us no rations other than cases of canned milk. Or was it, as some of the men grumbled, not really a mistake at all—the rear-echelon gangsters had diverted our tins of meat and other concentrated foods to the Paris black market. One thing was certain: carton after carton, no matter what it was labeled, contained nothing but cans of milk.

Sleep was the best defense against increasingly surly troops. In the crowded trucks, men huddled together for warmth, sharing coats and blankets, a few tired old veterans ministering with compassionate roughness to frightened recruits. The cold itself was terrifying, seducing all of us toward capitulation, toward unbroken, fatal, final sleep. Occasionally, after hours of silence and stillness from all the men in a lurching truck, someone would stir himself and beat the others into wakefulness. Men cracked. Some wept, some swore, some snarled.

A pale sun glinted off the snows during one of our infrequent stops for relief call. No houses or barns were in the immediate vicinity; yet, seemingly out of nowhere, ragged figures, like frosted specters, materialized beside us. Modest young soldiers fumbled with their trousers as starved women and emaciated children moved among them begging food and clothing. In the small group of peasants near me was a legless child on a handmade sled pulled by his older brother. Their mother had seen the tumbled cans of milk in our trucks, and asked if we could spare some for the infant in her arms. "My breasts are dry," she explained.

A sergeant—no better or worse than the rest of us, we had always believed—stepped forward and held an open tin before her. Each time the woman reached for it, he withdrew the can.

"You look amply endowed, little mother," he taunted. "Let use see if you're really dry."

With great dignity, the woman drew aside her worn, frayed shawl. Most of us stared at the ground. The sergeant lifted the can of milk to the woman's eyes, inverted it, and let its contents trickle slowly out, creating a slender, delicate channel in the snow at her feet.

Another soldier struck him, and fists flew. A hysterical lieutenant came on the run, ordering everyone back into the trucks. Motors roared, snow flew out from under spinning tires, and the peasants backed off to the edge of the road. I was jammed in over a tailgate and could see the shawled woman with her children. My eyes remained riveted on the dirty bandages covering the wounds of her legless son. Near them was the emptied tin of milk.

We have resumed our places, and the meal begins. Daria casts me a fleetingly guilty look as she takes the first sip from her replenished glass. Conversation begins—about school rooms, football, TV programs, business and social schedules, the high cost of living. The dog has wandered under the table and nudged my leg. I look down to see her red tongue take up the last few drops of milk from the floor.

A HALLOWEEN MASK or two are still about; though the day has come and gone, the smaller children continue to play ghost and goblin. I hear their hushed whispers, low moans and groans, and suppressed giggles as they creep up the stairway to surprise and scare me. I have been lying down reading, about Mexico's Halloween, the Day of the Dead, and anticipating an hour of late Sunday afternoon dozing. But the little masked witches climb my bed, pummel chest, stomach, and legs, chatter and fuss. I put aside the book and reluctantly surrender all chances for a nap.

We talk of ghosts. Daria feigns horror, not without a few cautious looks over her shoulder, but Chiara argues it's all kid stuff. Or mostly, maybe not entirely. For the children at school have told her about La Llorona, and maybe that one really does roam el rito's riverbed and the arroyos. Some of the boys and girls have sworn they heard her in Arroyo de los Chamisos, and grownups say she stalks the Capitol buildings at night. But there really aren't any ghosts, are there, Dad?

I'm looking at their great-grandmother's desk in the corner as they talk, and wondering how to answer them. That arrow-scarred chest had belonged to Ellen's grandfather's family; it crossed the country in a Conestoga. In the round faces before me, I see the delightful fusion of Mayflower and Mediterranean heritage, and am aware, as I usually am, of all who went before us and just how much they are still with us. How, without frightening the children, distinguish between ghost and spirit?

I try. Daria clucks away—witchy-poos are witchy-poos, lots of trick-or-treat fun and nothing more—but Chiara is attentive and reflective. "This book was Candy's?" she asks, incredulous, hardly able to believe books were published as long ago as her grandmother's childhood. "And you really do think of her whenever you see it?"

But this is all too difficult. The child soon gives up such concepts and returns to more titillating questions. "I mean real ghosts—have you ever seen a real ghost?"

Saved by the bell, for the phone is ringing. I abandon the girls to listen to a long monologue on community environmental problems and why I should sign the latest petition to save Santa Fe's historic character. Here, too, we are involved with those who have gone before us.

Later, at table, Ellen cautions us in our use of a platter, crazed and brown with age, which came to this country with my grandmother's trousseau. Chiara's eyes seek mine, and I see that she has remembered our earlier conversation, is poised on the threshold of that mysterious region where her ancestors somehow endure. But Ruan impatiently asks that she pass a biscuit, and we all set to the business of eating, and the moment is gone.

Once upon a time I lived all alone on a beach in California. I worked in a nearby ceramics studio, casting and decorating slick giftware for the mass market. During free hours I painted and wrote; I took no time for recreation or to make friends. One day at work, while handling acid, I severely burned the thumb and index finger of my right hand. Fellow employees took me to a doctor, who stripped the flesh from the fingers, treated and bandaged them, said their condition was bad and that amputation might prove necessary, set up a future appointment, and sent me home.

At first I could function, holding the injured, painful hand high while I cooked, ate, showered, and dressed with a clumsy left hand. But pain soon had me abed, the burning fingers plunged into a bucket of ice. I drifted in and out of consciousness, aware that I was in shock, feverish and without strength, too ill to get up. There was no phone, but I was not particularly alarmed. Though family and friends were at the opposite end of the continent, I felt sure that the landlord, the girl down the beach, or my employer would be dropping in to check. No one came.

Setting suns told me days were going by. I could see the golden-red reflections between slats of the slightly opened Venetian blinds. At other times, the room was completely black or bathed in a silvery gray half-light in which furnishings and walls took on ambiguous shapes. At all times I heard the ocean. Though I knew that the beach was wide and even during the highest tides kept the sea at a safe distance, now it sounded as if waves were crashing against my door.

There were few moments of consciousness. When they did come, I vaguely sensed that pain and fever had made me delirious, and that nothing I thought, saw, or heard could be trusted. The voice of the sea was as seductive as Ulysses' sirens; if I had been able to rise from the mast of my bed, I might have walked into her arms. Finally, I despaired that anyone would come, and lay waiting to fall back into merciful oblivion.

I woke to a sunset that flooded the room blood-red. And the walls seemed expanded, boundless, the room large enough to house everyone I had ever loved. I was aware of their presence and solicitude, tangible only in a semicircle of shadow around the bed; aware also, gradually, of one recognizable figure. It was my grandfather, dead before I was five, who now reached out a hand, as tenderly and gayly as ever, assuring me that all would be well, urging me to get up. I savored every moment of the encounter, but I do not know how long it lasted, or how and when it ended.

In the morning, the pain had subsided and my fever was gone. I ate, dressed, and took a bus to the doctor's office. He treated me, redressed the hand, and sent me on my way.

Chiara is on my lap, relaying still another report of La Llorona's having been heard wailing through the night in still another Santa Fe arroyo. And have you ever really seen a ghost? And if you really did, weren't you afraid? The blunted tip of my index finger tingles with sensitivity as I stroke the child's hair. We are back to the problem of ghost versus spirit, and how do I adequately explain it to her? Perhaps one should write it down.

NOVEMBER

Whose world were we in,
and what was real?

T HE PLANE is not crowded. I have a window seat with no immediate neighbors, the rare luxury of solitude and nothing to do.
Sunlight streams through the glass, warming bodies chilled by the
early, severe winter. Below spotty clouds, I see the Sangres crowned
white with glinting snows, study the hydrography of the range's peaks
—waterways, ritos, arroyos, frozen already, not to cascade into valley
and Rio until distant spring.

Out from over New Mexico, the cloud cover is solid. Stewardesses
are serving breakfast, and most of the passengers are in animated conversation. They are an international group, speaking many languages,
and are in holiday mood. The pilot confirms this impression over the
intercom, welcoming aboard the world's first champion hot-air bal-
loonist and his fellow contestants from the recent runs at Albuquerque.
The balloonists are a happy crew, and I smile at the warm invitation of
one of them to join him at their end of the cabin. But I remain alone
with sober thoughts, going home again.

Thomas Wolfe said you can't do that. I know now that I have
disagreed with him for years, that I have had more than one home—
physical and spiritual— and that I can go back. Literary men are
crowding my mind. Wolfe gives way to James Agee and the title of his
fine book *A Death in the Family*. The jet is winging me east to the
Chesapeake, to people and places of my boyhood, to a world that has

radically changed since I was part of it. But change cannot alter what is timeless, and I am thinking of what I shared with a kid sister whom I go now to bury—and how that is part of me, and perhaps of my issue, for eternity.

How close we always were: in age, temperament, dreams, in mischief and daring, and in sorrows. She was one of my dearest childhood companions, and it was never a sacrifice to desert athletic fields and run off on an adventure with Jetta. Two years younger than I, she allowed me to lead; but with all the wisdom of the feminine mystique, she channeled my captaincy toward unselfish goals, pursuits we equally relished. We were often two against the world, not only the world of adults but the world of our peers; and our greatest pleasure was to escape together into adventures big and small that no one else could share. How many of these have I, with a fickle memory, forgotten— and lost forever now that she is no longer around to speak of them.

This morning I soar above the earth (and she is with me), but as children it was trains we rode. Our father was a railroad man, and in my pocket were passes to take us away from Baltimore, wherever, whenever we wished to go. I was not yet a teenager when I was traveling alone to the great east-coast cities, beginning my life-long love affair with Manhattan. At some point, I persuaded my parents that I was responsible enough to take my little sister with me on these day excursions. Off we would go, Depression children with transportation guaranteed but little change in our pockets. We would rise before dawn, walk miles through the streets of Baltimore to Penn Station, ride a Washington-New York express for four and a half hours, and plunge into Seventh Avenue and Times Square with a fearlessness natural only to children.

We knew the city like natives and were wise to its wealth of free attractions: Central Park, window shopping, people-watching, museums, Washington Square and the Battery, Fifth Avenue parades and open-air concerts or theater. We hiked from one end of the island to the other, sometimes blue with cold, always excited, exhilarated at this best of classrooms and playgrounds. Pint-sized movie-buffs, we more often than not sacrificed lunch money ("don't tell Mother") to 10-cent admissions for the last balcony of the Astor and films no one else would take us to see—the great cinema art of Garbo's *Camille*, Wendy Hiller's *Pygmalion*, Chaplin's *The Great Dictator*. If we lingered too long, late trains got us home well after dark. Anxious parents swore "Never again." But they recognized in us, I believe, an unusual maturity and a sense of responsibility—and a hunger for freedom, which, if not cautiously monitored and encouraged, might erupt into revolution. After a short while, we were off on another excursion.

Her name was Concetta, and I am thinking now how she, disliking formality, fought against my preference for it instead of the diminutive, Jetta. TWA now picks up my breakfast tray, and I remember a diner—chrome, plastic, and bad lighting—where she and I broke bread together in our first communion after the war. Her fiancé had been shot down over Britain: I wore no Purple Heart but was wounded beyond understanding. We were casualties without official badges, and no one could see. The hands we joined that night remained permanently joined—miles, marriages, children, and totally diverse ways of life never broke the bond. We had only to look into each others' eyes, after long separations, to know the magic was still there.

We are descending over Chicago, lost between heaven and earth in a solid bank of heavy cloud. For many minutes, the plane remains suspended in a celestial universe of infinite whiteness and purity. It is an uncomfortably long interim for a few of the balloonists. "How strange," one says. "Eerie," his wife replies. Another literary memory prods me—*Outward Bound*. Who wrote it? But I am strangely at peace—knowing precisely where I am, what this journey is, and whose hand I have held throughout.

FOR A BRIEF period as a very young child, I intensely disliked my Christian name. Surrounded by Toms, Dicks, and Harrys in the classroom, by Joes and Jims and Bills on the school playground, I smarted under the formality of Andrew. When family and friends labeled me with various uninventive nicknames, I welcomed and encouraged the prosaic appellations. It was my father's mother, adamant in addressing me with the full and proper name, who first kindled my pride and acceptance of it.

Long years were to pass, however, before I developed an interest in my patron, Andrew the fisherman from Bethsaida. He is infrequently mentioned in scripture, and was always overshadowed by his brother · Simon Peter or friend John. Popular legends about Andrew are few, and we tend to lump him casually among the Twelve, rarely singling him out for special attention. Almost the only kinship I felt with him for a long time was a shared love of the sea, coastal waters, lakes and rivers. And, appropriately, it was a boatman, ferrying me across the white-capped channel at Bocca de Magra, who triggered my curiosity to know more about the first Apostle.

The boatman was old, gnarled, and wrinkled, but he anchored huge bare feet firmly in the bow of the small barque and rowed with a powerful stroke. He ignored his two passengers, Paul and me, preferring to gaze back at the sparkling marbles in the peaks of Carrara or ahead to a few hovels dotting the beach at Magra. Only when we had offered him wine and exchanged introductions was his tolerance of foreigners displaced with interest.

"Andrea," he said. "That, too, is my name."

After I jokingly suggested that we shared a patron who got but short shrift in the Bible—"neglected men, these Andrews"—he wagged a disapproving finger at me. And when he spoke, it was into the elements, his words flung before him out over the water and carried back to us on the wind.

There is merit in being left out of things, he said in that austere dialect of Liguria. The first shall be the last. Is it possible that you

Americani have not been taught that Andrew was the first of the Twelve to recognize the Master in a stranger, and to follow Him? This event took place beside the Jordan, where Andrew was standing with his friend John the Baptist when the Nazarene approached them. Man of friendship, not neglect, is how we think of Andrew in the Mediterranean.

Consider, *Americano*. Practically every scriptural reference to Andrew places him among friends; or has him bringing friends to the Master, only to retire as others take prominence. That is what happened with his own brother Simon, called Peter; with the disciples James and John, with the boy carrying loaves and fishes at the Sea of Galilee. A Greek seaman I knew, himself called Andreas, tells me there were Greeks at the Feast of Passover who had heard of the Nazarene and wanted to meet Him. Strangers to Jewish customs, they sought out the shy Philip and asked for introductions. But Philip turned to Andrew, friend and go-between, and it was Andrew who arranged a meeting. Greeks to this day insist that Andrew introduced them to Christ.

Our boat had touched shore, and Paul and I reached for lire to pay the old man. He seemed abstracted, and we had to guide the money to his pocket.

"It's true, as you say," the boatman muttered. "He was left out of things—not called with Peter, James, and John to witness the healing of Jairus' daughter, or to the Transfiguration or Gethsemane. But isn't the grace to be left out, taken for granted, an important part of love and friendship? We often reserve such behavior for those we love and trust most, while feeling obliged to court less worthy associates who weakly suffer from intentional and unintentional neglect."

Without a backward glance, we left the old sailor-philosopher talking to himself as we hurried across the beach. I could not know then that this stranger, occupying a half-hour of my life with talk of a saint easily left behind, would linger in my mind so long as I lived. When late November and the feast of Andrew roll around, I remember the boatman.

Even more curious. This year I speak of him to a librarian who immediately accuses me of fabricating a tale based on a medieval poem, *Andreas,* which she says bears a closer relationship to *Beowulf* than any other Old English writings. I have never heard of the work, but the first friend to whom I mention it goes to his book shelves and hands me a copy of Charles W. Kennedy's *Early English Christian Poetry.* My embarrassment at ignorance of this great epic poem has been displaced by the joy of discovery. Now, as the feast nears, I read the translation of *Andreas,* accompanying the saint in a "broad-beamed boat" en route to rescue Matthew from the cannibals of Mermedonia. Nowhere in the long poem is language more beautiful than in Andrew's conversation with the Boatman—who proves to be, in the anonymous author's grand cadences, Great Leader on the Ocean-Highway, Warden of the Wave, Helm of All Creatures, Sovereign of Men.

RIFLING THROUGH a file of drawings earmarked for eventual framing, I turn up a small sketch in colored inks of the Santa Fe plaza. Its bright splashes and energetic lines, almost obliterating subject matter, tell me at once it is an Alfred Morang, acquired many years ago, and the only Morang we have. My mother-in-law purchased it for us one festive day in front of the Palace of the Governors, where Alfred was producing sketches for the tourist trade.

The first Alfred Morang I ever saw was a small oil, riotous in color, heavy with impasto, explosive with emotion. It was typical of his work at that time (1954), free and very bold—and disturbing. Whether one liked it or not, one could not easily ignore it. Three heavily rouged harlots, arms linked together, stood against a Santa Fe night-scene and glared indolently at the spectator. Garish oranges and reds twisted frantically through predominant blues, and the women of the painting seemed bathed in writhing firelight.

"Ladies of the Evening," he called them when I later mentioned the picture to Alfred. He had done a series on the theme, and he managed to find a few others to show me. They were equally provocative, each executed with vigorous brush strokes and palette knife, fusing tenderness and violence, each somehow a definitive statement despite these obviously conflicting elements.

I never saw much of Alfred. He lived alone near us and occasionally dropped in to review our work. Slight, full of nervous energy, the Vandyke beard poised jauntily before him, he would move from painting to painting, singling out what he liked. His weekly column of art criticism in the *New Mexican* was carefully and conscientiously written, free of cant and personal bias.

The columns were only a small part of his compulsive writing. I visited his cluttered rooms a few times and found manuscripts and parts of manuscripts stacked or scattered over every available surface. Like his paintings, they were original and difficult, a world unto themselves, haunted by a wild yet gentle beauty. I remember that one day the wind was roaring through an open window, and pages of manuscript tumbled, swirled, and eddied everywhere, over our heads and about our ankles. I knew a moment of panic at seeing those thousands of words scattered on the wind, but Alfred was feeding a kitten and seemed oblivious to the blizzard of prose.

He had one of Santa Fe's first radio talk-shows, and on a few occasions he invited me to be a guest. The last time I faced him over a microphone, he was very ill, and the table at which we sat rattled under his convulsive trembling. But his courage never failed. The interview was professional, and not without humor.

Though we saw less and less of him socially as domestic and business concerns claimed us, I frequently glimpsed Alfred on his innumerable Canyon Road errands. More often than not, he was bundled in a long black coat, whiskers white with frost, paintings under one arm. He walked quickly, bent into the weather, and most of the time appeared indifferent to his surroundings. Speaking to him triggered inevitable, and often brilliant, discourses on whatever painting, literature, or music occupied his mind at the moment. He was recognized on sight by most Santa Feans and enjoyed the rather dubious honor of official representative of the art colony.

I was in the neighborhood bar the night his house caught fire. An old army buddy from Chicago had come to town and wanted to down cognac while viewing local color. There was little of that to view, for it was a bitterly cold night; the streets were deserted, the bar was almost empty and quite cheerless. My bachelor friend dredged up memories of a thousand other cafés in France and Germany, while my thoughts strayed to demands at home. Three weary women at the other end of the long bar seemed to be nowhere, waiting for nothing.

The sound of sirens startled us all. Fire engines skidded past the door. We could hear them screeching to a halt in a compound behind the bar. I knew Alfred's small adobe casita was there.

Nothing could be done. The roof had already crashed in, and flames leaped high in the sky. I was thinking how very, very strange it was to be standing beside this war comrade watching helplessly, just as we had done in Europe, as property and life were devoured by fire. And ever stranger—later—when stretcher carriers fled the still-burning ruin and rested their burden on the frozen ground; for firelight, like streaks of red and yellow pigment, crawled erratically over the sad tableau. And looking up from the bearded profile on the stretcher, I saw that the women from the bar had joined us. Harsh, bright colors spiraled over their tawdry dress and hennaed hair, highlighting them against the black night. They were exactly like the three women in his painting, bewildered and pathetic, vulnerable under the heavy crust of cosmetics. His Ladies of the Evening.

Whose world were we in, and what was real? But my army friend would have none of that, and we walked home silently in the cold.

TRAVELING ALONE at this point in life can present a rare opportunity for freedom from work pressures, conferences, the demands of professional associates and friends, the needs of children—a chance to slow down, stop and stare, think a little, put aside, if only briefly, responsibility. For a few hours, responsibility belongs to pilot and crew. The 727 soars high above foams of cloud obscuring the earth, negating man's successes, as well as his failures, upon its topography, freeing passengers from land-locked concerns that are meaningless in this vast expanse of sky. Forget the homework brought along for airborne study, close one's eyes, and savor the limbo.

It works on the 727. But after Denver, I transfer to a Convair 580, which puddle-jumps all over Kansas, flying at a greatly reduced altitude, buffeted by turbulence. My drowsing is interrupted by the frequent descents to isolated prairie communities, and I try in vain to recapture escape. The passenger beside me guarantees that I will not.

Though the plane boasts other empty seats, she had elected, upon boarding at Denver, to crowd into one beside me. She is obviously a veteran of this particular route, and quickly advises me, "If you want a drink, order it immediately after takeoff, while we're still in Colorado. The skies over Kansas are dry." This intriguingly brusque suggestion prompts me to take a closer look at her.

In her middle years, trim, smartly outfitted in a pantsuit for casual travel, the woman is blatantly efficient. Within minutes, she has handed me a business card heralding the firm for which she and her husband are regional distributors. That organizational name is blazoned also across the face of a pack of matches kept handy as she ravenously consumes cigarettes. After the frequent landings and takeoffs, during which smoking is prohibited, she waits tensely for the signal lifting restriction, then strikes a match with a sigh of relief. Her hands are rarely still, toying with the incendiaries, the cigarette, the plastic tumbler of bourbon.

"My husband had business in Utah," she volunteers, "but I couldn't go along for his trip. So he flew west and I'm taking off east

—going home again. Every once in a while, I've got to go home to Kansas."

I am looking down on the flatness of the land and, perhaps insensitively, remark that mountains and deserts have accustomed me to more dramatic landscapes. The woman's reply is tinged with offense.

"Oh, the mountains are beautiful, but life since I've left the plains has been little but hard work, grubbing. Business is a 24-hour-day affair. It's all a rat race, and I keep thinking what Kansas was, its slow pace, when I was a little girl. My hometown hasn't changed all that much. I go home and sit with Mama, and it's like the world's stood still."

She nurses her drink jealously, sipping it very slowly. "I'd like another, but not at these prices. Inflation. Air fares being what they are, you'd think we'd be offered complimentary cocktails." She calls my attention to every vibration of the plane, every noise in its cabin. Her heavily ringed fingers are white-knuckled around the tumbler. When the stewardess puts plastic-wrapped sandwiches before us, my companion deftly lifts one piece of chicken from between meager slabs of bread, then pushes the remainder of the snack aside. She lights a fresh cigarette and sucks at the watery bourbon.

"They're for my little daughters," I explain when she asks why I've pocketed unused packets of salt and pepper along with the garish cocktail-stirrers. Quickly discouraging any further mention of domesticity, or children, she talks about her secretary, a jewel of a career-person upon whom she can absolutely depend whenever these trips back to the fountainhead seem necessary. There is a pet toy terrier to be cared for during these absences, a dear sweet thing that dislikes commercial kennels; and the secretary is an admirable dog-watcher. Before the terrier, there was another canine, a devoted animal full of love, but she died.

I try closing my eyes. Where now is the 727, altitudes of 30,000 feet, empty neighboring seats, escape? What is the caste mark or professional brand stamped upon my brow shouting, "Listener. Talk to him"? I let the drones of voice and plane merge, a cacophony of sound from which fatigue mercifully manufactures a lullaby. I slip out of bounds for a few precious minutes, into the safe, still arms of Morpheus.

"We've won the regional distributors' award," the voice comes back, "and the firm's sending us to Hawaii. First time out of the country for my husband and me. It's time we saw something different, you know. All these years of grind, pressure, competition, my running home to Kansas. He says it's time to cut strings, not look back but look forward, find new beginnings. Maybe in Hawaii. We'll be there December first."

I am not fully awake. My response is spontaneous, totally unguarded. "Very appropriate and symbolic—the first day of Advent and a new liturgical year, the promise of Yahweh."

The woman stares at me in alarm. Then very slowly she begins to raise a shoulder as she turns her back, blocking the madman from view. I am left undisturbed for the rest of the flight.

THE CHILDREN greet changes of season with anticipation. They leave summer behind with no regrets, looking forward not only to New Mexico's glorious autumn but to the long cold winter of her high country. They take astonishingly casual leave of the hot sun, shirt-sleeve weather, and their lazy days in warm, sheltered patios; they speak excitingly of the first snows, the frigid hikes to school, the sledding down slopes, and the snowball fights.

Of course, the change for them holds forth tantalizing prizes in the traditional holidays of Thanksgiving, Christmas, and the New Year. Impatient to grow, to get on with their lives, to celebrate fully each new day of wonder, they forge breathlessly ahead from season to season with hardly a backward glance.

Watching them as we work at garden cleanup chores under a bright sky, I know that I cannot so easily look forward to winter. It is not simply that I prefer warmth to cold or blossoms to dormant trees and shrubs. It is more a reluctance to go forward without pause; it is the need for some few hours to stop and look back and evaluate. Nature herself moves slowly, often imperceptibly, while modern man dashes without reflection through one of her seasons after another. Our agrarian ancestors knew the value of pacing one's life to the tempo of the land, to the swells and falls of natural rhythm. Few of us today abandon personal treadmills long enough to give time or thought to where we have been or where we are headed while the clock races.

Or if we do, it is frequently, as has been the case these past few years, to indulge in false nostalgias, empty yearnings for the good old days with their grand old times, which never really existed. Tunes and clothing of yesteryear, romantic novels and movies evoke a soft-focused Depression or wartime; Broadway musicals glamorize with pastel lighting and full string-section the harsh eras of organized crime, racial privation, overseas battlegrounds, social revolutions. The past was never so rosy, never quite so innocent as we like to fantasize; and to remember it that way is to profit us nothing toward the future.

A young college student recently advised me that neither past nor future was worth thinking about—the present's where it's at, where the action is, where we're all strung out, and in which we must get it all together. I am not easily provoked into debate with the young, but I did wonder aloud how we would manage to get it together without some acknowledgement of the lessons of history, the study of civilizations and cultures, a sense of identity in heritage and tradition. My companion had little patience or sympathy for anything but his own generation. He pointed out, irrefutably, that some of my dearest friends are casualties to years long since vanished, trapped in the beliefs and customs prevalent when they came of age. He mentioned the octogenarian in her home of Victorian antiques, conversationally rummaging—however charmingly—through the attics of a dead turn-of-the-century America; the aged flapper, still so Clara Bowish, still the coquettish Fitzgerald heroine, the faded bohemian; a businessman we know holding on to snobbish suburban caste values—country clubs, gentlemen's agreements regarding race, creed, and color—no longer tolerable; the balding veterans sharing with complacent wives *gemütlich* evenings over rums and cokes, Glenn Miller records, and faded snapshots. What has any of this to do with the post-bomb, Watergate world of population explosion, rampant pollution, space, and the Moral Revolution?

One concedes the boy has a point—or several. But cultural casualties are no newer under the sun than anything else. I suggest (and he nods concurrence) that thirty, forty, fifty years from now a few of his contemporaries will have proven themselves foot-draggers, muttering a jargon long obsolete and languishing among the hip, psychedelic accoutrements and fashions that a future world can only label anachronistic.

If not nostalgia or an easy acquiescence to a hedonistic present that negates past and future, what then? Daria, assisting with the garden chores, helps me rediscover an old truth. She wants to know if corn and squash grow everywhere—along the eastern seaboard where grandparents live, south on the Rio or in California where siblings attend college—or only in Santa Fe. We find ourselves discussing corn as an ancient Indian crop, sacred to the pueblo peoples, and I remember again (as always, with surprise) that this child is a native New Mexican. And what a glorious tangle of people and events produced her— maternal heritage cradled in the Mayflower and the American Revolution, paternal reaching back to the Mediterranean, her birthright giving her claim to this mystical land of the cacique and the conquistador. She is unique because of those who went before her, and one is obliged to tell her some of the old stories, to let her know who she is and encourage her to take pride in that.

Lóng before the advent of television, when family tales were repeated around my parents' kitchen table, I chided my mother for harking back so frequently on days gone by. She responded with an old saying that her father had learned from his father in Sorrento and passed on to his children in the New World: "The past, well digested, helps us stomach the present; and that gives us an appetite for the future."